T5-AQQ-708

GOSHEN COLLEGE LIBRARY
GOSHEN, INDIANA

LIFE WORLD LIBRARY

FRANCE

TIME LIFE BOOKS

LIFE WORLD LIBRARY

LIFE NATURE LIBRARY

LIFE SCIENCE LIBRARY

THE LIFE HISTORY OF THE UNITED STATES

GREAT AGES OF MAN

TIME-LIFE LIBRARY OF ART

TIME READING PROGRAM

INTERNATIONAL BOOK SOCIETY

LIFE Pictorial Atlas of the World

The Epic of Man

The Wonders of Life on Earth

The World We Live In

The World's Great Religions

The LIFE Book of Christmas

LIFE'S Picture History of Western Man

The LIFE Treasury of American Folklore

America's Arts and Skills

300 Years of American Painting

The Second World War

LIFE'S Picture History of World War II

Picture Cook Book

LIFE Guide to Paris

914.4
B78f
c.3

DC
29
B 7,3

91926

LIFE WORLD LIBRARY

FRANCE

by D. W. Brogan

and The Editors of LIFE

TIME INCORPORATED   NEW YORK

GOSHEN COLLEGE LIBRARY
GOSHEN, INDIANA

COVER: Sheep graze on flats
near the magnificent medieval
abbey of Mont-St.-Michel, which
rises on its historic island
off the coast of France.

ABOUT THE WRITER

Sir Denis Brogan, Professor of Political Science at Cambridge University, is a distinguished historian and a recognized authority on both the United States and France. He was born in Scotland and educated at Oxford, Harvard and the University of Glasgow. Known to the literary world as D. W. Brogan, he is the author of 16 books, as well as innumerable magazine articles and essays on international affairs. His *France Under the Republic,* published in 1940, is regarded as a definitive work on prewar France.

In the text chapters of this volume, Sir Denis provides an interpretation of France based on his long acquaintance with the country. For many years he and his wife, who is an archeologist, have summered in the Auvergne region of central France. A Chevalier of the French Legion of Honor and a member of the Institut de France, he holds honorary doctorates from four French universities.

France © 1960, 1966 Time Inc. All rights reserved. Published simultaneously in Canada.
Library of Congress catalogue card number 60-16445.
School and library distribution by Silver Burdett Company.

Contents

TIME-LIFE BOOKS

EDITOR
Norman P. Ross
EXECUTIVE EDITOR
Maitland A. Edey
TEXT DIRECTOR   ART DIRECTOR
Jerry Korn   Edward A. Hamilton
CHIEF OF RESEARCH
Beatrice T. Dobie
Assistant Text Director: Harold C. Field
Assistant Art Director: Arnold C. Holeywell
Assistant Chiefs of Research:
Monica O. Horne, Martha Turner

•

PUBLISHER
Rhett Austell
General Manager: Joseph C. Hazen Jr.
Planning Director: Frank M. White
Business Manager: John D. McSweeney
Circulation Director: Joan D. Manley
Publishing Board: Nicholas Benton, Louis Bronzo,
James Wendell Forbes, John S. Wiseman

LIFE MAGAZINE

EDITOR: Edward K. Thompson
MANAGING EDITOR: George P. Hunt
PUBLISHER: Jerome S. Hardy

LIFE WORLD LIBRARY

SERIES EDITOR: Oliver E. Allen
Editorial Staff for *France:*
Designer: Leonard Jossel
Chief Researcher: Grace Brynolson
Researchers: Irene S. Ertugrul, Renée S. Pickèl,
Lucy Collier, Madeleine Richards, Paula von Haimberger Arno,
Mary Elizabeth Davidson, Gwyneth Barger

EDITORIAL PRODUCTION
Color Director: Robert L. Young
Copy Staff: Marian Gordon Goldman, Patricia Miller,
Dolores A. Littles
Picture Bureau: Margaret K. Goldsmith, Merry Mass
Art Assistants: Douglas B. Graham, Arthur Solin,
John M. Woods

The text for the chapters of this book was written by D. W. Brogan.
Valuable help in producing the volume was provided by the following
individuals and departments of Time Inc.: Alfred Eisenstaedt, Eliot
Elisofon, Yale Joel and Dmitri Kessel, LIFE staff photographers; Doris
O'Neil, Chief, LIFE Picture Library; Richard M. Clurman, Chief, TIME-
LIFE News Service; Peter Draz, Chief, Bureau of Editorial Reference.

Introduction

This volume on France, with its interpretive text by the distinguished British historian D. W. Brogan and its excellent accompanying picture essays, should have a particular appeal to American readers.

A strain of affectionate sentiment has, since our Revolutionary days, generally characterized the American attitude toward France, and has survived periods of mutual irritation and even of incomprehension.

It is impossible, in reading the Brogan narrative, not to marvel anew at the rich panorama of French history, with its complex mixture of glory and vicissitude. In spite of innumerable internal dissensions and external conflicts, this homogeneous people has maintained, throughout the centuries, an almost unparalleled cohesion against foreign pressures.

In no other country is the right of individual expression so indulgently cherished, or the dignity of the individual so tenaciously respected, even when the consequences have occasionally approached political anarchy.

The French character and sense of national purpose have been fundamentally unchanged by spectacular victories or defeats; the "sweetness of life" there has been little affected by transient misfortunes. Slow to adapt their policies to changes in balance of military power, these proud people have cultivated their own incomparable garden and retained their dominant cultural influence in western civilization.

Ideas still flow from them as if from an inexhaustible spring. Not the least interesting of Professor Brogan's observations are those on the birth and growth of the principle of European unity, fathered by Jean Monnet in France. Expressed thus far chiefly in economic terms, this principle nonetheless represents one of the most significant and unusual political philosophies of our age.

After a period of stagnation following the ravages of the first World War, and accentuated in the aftermath of the second, the renascence of France has occurred in almost miraculous fashion, to the benefit of all humanity.

DAVID K. E. BRUCE

former U.S. Ambassador to France

After a sudden storm the Place de la Concorde's broad pavements glisten under the onrushing traffic. Here, where not

a fountain stands, King Louis XVI was guillotined in 1793.

1

A Nation Both Ancient and Young

THE American who sails on a French ship from New York realizes the moment he gets on board that he has become the guest of a civilization that is very old and at the same time highly modern. The ship itself is a product of the electronic age. Radar, radio, transocean telephones, movies and air conditioning are part of the international technical culture in which the United States is a leader. But although the ship is so palpably part of that modern world, it is also part of another, older world. Messages are delivered by hand as well as by telephone. There are tapestries that may be new, but are products of an age-old art. Wood paneling conceals the steel framework.

The American will land, too, in the port of Le Havre, which in its harbor installations as well as in its appearance is for the most part modern. Both Le Havre and Cherbourg were badly battered in the last war and therefore have had to be completely reconstructed. But even in the ports, and still more outside the ports, the old is as prominent as the new. The average age of houses in Normandy, the province that the traveler passes through on his way to Paris, is 140 years. Many are more than 300 years old.

A railway system that has the fastest locomotives in the world may be whisking the American to Paris, but he is whisked past a landscape in which most man-made objects are old. The new school or bridge or house is set in a background of antiquity. The general pattern of the villages, the pattern of the farms in some cases, was settled before Columbus discovered America. The most up-to-date techniques have to live alongside a habit of mind that is not sure that novelty is a good thing in itself. Some of the fields will seem small, and they are. The farms may be small and the farmer may be performing many different functions, raising cereal crops and root crops, chickens, cattle and possibly even horses, all on an area no bigger than a big Iowa field planted in a single crop. But he will almost certainly be using some modern machinery; he may have a tractor or a car; he may have television. He lives, with some discomfort, in several centuries at once. He is moving or being pushed into the 20th Century, but he is far less certain than his American counterpart that this is desirable.

THE real story of France today is the fight between the old, the pleasant and the accepted and the new modern world which France has entered, with one half of the country rejoicing and the other half lamenting the death of the traditional France that had settled all questions long ago. For what is true of the farmer is true of the representative Frenchman. He is mechanically ingenious, like an American, but he may use his ingenuity to make an old tool live a second life, instead of scrapping it for a new one.

The same mixed impression will be given at the airports or the great railway stations in Paris. The stations, although somewhat modernized, are basically the same structures Mark Twain

admired nearly a hundred years ago. In Paris itself there will be a whirlpool of traffic to startle even a New Yorker, but much of it will pour through streets as narrow as any in Boston, for although the broad boulevards of the city were laid out roughly a hundred years ago the majority of the streets are far older. Of all the great cities of the world, Paris has changed the least in this century. Only now, in the new underpasses that attempt to cope with the strangling traffic and in some new office buildings, are there signs of the second half of the 20th Century.

PARIS is, of course, the central jewel of the French crown. But for many centuries Frenchmen have admired their country and the outside world has shared that admiration. It has been a long time since the French first referred to *la douce France* (sweet France) and then to *la belle France* (beautiful France). They have long rejoiced in the astonishing variety of scenery, climate and resources. Only the climate and products of the deep tropics and the climate of areas like the Dakotas or Siberia are absent from the French spectrum. And this great variety of natural resources is available in a remarkably compact country that is smaller than Texas. The French people, who greatly admire mathematical elegance, sometimes refer to their country as a hexagon, which it roughly is. They are proud that France has shape as well as variety.

Geography favors France in other ways. The country's principal navigable river system, that of the Seine, is connected by canal with other rivers. Paris has good communications with all parts of France and is also one of the greatest inland ports in Europe. The other great rivers have other assets. The Rhône dashes out of Lake Geneva on its rush to the Mediterranean with too great a drop to be naturally navigable, but that same drop makes it admirable for the generation of hydroelectric power. The Dordogne and the Garonne Rivers, which join to make the Gironde estuary in southwest France, are important because on their banks are some of the most famous vineyards in the world. The Rhine, to the east, is a French frontier river, and the joint exploitation of its resources for navigation and power by France and West Germany is one of the notable signs of the times.

Two other frontiers are guarded by magnificent mountains: the Alps separate France from Switzerland and Italy, and the Pyrenees mark the border of Spain. France has in Mont Blanc the highest mountain in western Europe. But the characteristic French landscape is not the dramatic heights of the Alps and the Pyrenees. It is the sunny, vine-clad hills or the great plains, which are usually framed with forests. Nearly a quarter of France is forest. Paris is surrounded by the great forests which were the hunting parks of the French kings: Fontainebleau, Compiègne, Chantilly, Rambouillet, each with its great castle in the center of the woods.

And this country around Paris is familiar to all the western world, for it has probably been the subject of more great paintings than any other area in the world. Its villages, its meadows, groves and streams have been painted by renowned artists for more than a hundred years. It is no wonder that Macaulay, the English historian, wrote of "... thy corn-fields green, and sunny vines, oh pleasant land of France!"

OF course the perfection of this land is very largely the work of men's hands. The forests have been planted and tended. The fields have been laid out, the rivers embanked for a very long time past. But the more obvious works of men's hands are equally varied and enchanting. France is the home of Gothic architecture. From France in the Middle Ages architects, masons and sculptors fanned out all over Europe. If Frenchmen were asked to choose the greatest architectural glory of France they would probably name the Cathedral of Chartres, which rises like a great ship out of the fertile wheatlands of the Beauce, southwest of Paris. But at the other end of France there is the equally astonishing red brick Cathedral of Ste.-Cécile at Albi, austere as a fortress on the outside and like a jewel box inside.

It is not only a matter of Gothic. There are magnificent prehistoric relics in France like the great alleyways of standing stones in Brittany. There are Roman theaters and temples like the Maison Carrée at Nîmes, which Thomas Jefferson admired so much that he made it the model for the Virginia state capitol in Richmond. There are great Romanesque churches in Auvergne, Burgundy and Languedoc, designed in the days before Gothic. There are great castles in all styles, fortresses of the Middle Ages like Carcassonne and Renaissance palaces like Chenonceaux and Chambord. There is the vastest of royal palaces at Versailles, and Paris is one of the greatest museums of architecture in the world, with everything from a Roman amphitheater to the experiments of Le Corbusier and his disciples. Here is richness.

THE tourist, indeed the resident in France, suffers from what the French call an *embarras de richesses* (an embarrassment of riches), and he is wise to begin by noting that the great dividing line is between the North and the South, with the Loire River as a kind of Mason-Dixon Line. South of the Loire is the country of grapevines, orange trees and olive groves, and of the mulberry trees that sustain the silkworms. Here people in towns like Perpignan really do dance spontaneously in the streets. Here is what the French call the *Midi*, literally the "midday," where the sun is theoretically always shining.

Here for more than a century northern Europeans and Americans have been coming to escape their own winters, and more recently to enjoy the long summers. But not many tourists notice that the long dry summers that are wonderful for developing a sun tan are bad for cattle, that the steep picturesque hills are hard to cultivate, and that the rivers which tumble so pleasantly down the valleys cannot be used for transportation as can the rivers of the North.

The French South, like the American South, has many modern areas and many centers of progress, but—again like the American South—it is for the most part poor economically and somehow out of the stream of things. Meanwhile the France of today, the France of prosperity and progress, is the French North.

In the South the tourist will notice that the people are "typical Frenchmen." They are shorter, darker and chunkier than the Frenchmen of northern France. They do all the things that foreign visitors expect of Frenchmen. They talk a great deal and talk very loudly. The northern French are full of stories of the boasting, vanity and verbal extravagance of the men from the South. The Southerners like to live in public and to conduct most human affairs in the street. The typical *Méridional* (man of the *Midi*) has been exhibited to the world again and again by the French comedian Fernandel.

It is surely not accidental that although the French national anthem, the most famous patriotic song in the world, was written in the mercantile Alsatian city of Strasbourg, it got its name from the fiery militiamen of Marseilles, who sang it while marching north to Paris on their way to dethrone King Louis XVI in 1792. The song is called "The Marseillaise." What else could it be called?

But the romantic countryside and the romantic people conceal from the tourist some depressing facts about the French South. And they also divert attention from some impressive facts about the drabber, flatter, but so much more promising North. Life is hard in the South. Many picturesque villages have far fewer people in them than they had a century ago.

Of course not all of the South is poor. Some areas have always been rich—particularly the Bordeaux wine-growing region in the southwest—and some other areas are becoming rich.

Nor is all of the North rich. The jagged peninsula of Brittany, which juts out into the Atlantic, is bleak and poor, a kind of Maine without the forests. Brittany's only great power resource is the potential of the River Rance estuary, whose great tides are being harnessed to produce hydroelectric power. Isolated parts of the northeast are poor and empty. In the main, however, the great fertile plains of the North are the heart of France.

The people of the North and South differ as much from each other as their geographies do. Northerners are as a rule bigger and blonder, more taciturn, more self-contained. In a province like Normandy they often look English. In the eastern provinces they often look German.

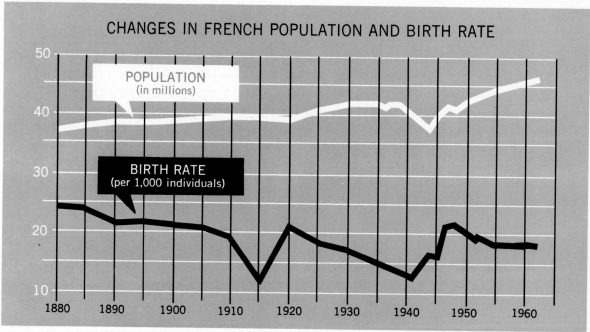

FLUCTUATING GROWTH of France is shown since 1880. The birth rate drop between 1910 and 1915 and after World War I was offset in population by the return of Alsace-Lorraine to France and by immigration. But immigration slowed in the 1930s and population fell. The birth rate climb since 1942 has brought steady population gains.

They eat more and drink more than the people of the *Midi*. They are more conservative in politics (outside the great cities) and less given to rhetoric than the Southerners. But the Frenchman from Dunkerque on the North Sea is as French as the Frenchman from Marseilles. They share a common culture and a common history and are both involved in the destiny of France.

THE most novel feature of that destiny is the sudden upswing in the French birth rate. In 1800 France was the most populous country in Europe outside Russia and about two thirds as populous as Russia itself. But from 1815 the birth rate began to fall, and in the first half of this century the French population was kept stable at around 40 million only by massive immigration. As a people the French, especially after the dreadful losses in both the great wars (1,400,000 in the first, 600,000 in the second), seemed doomed to a permanent decline. But starting in 1942 the French birth rate reversed its trend. It is now higher than in most of the other countries of western Europe, and France will soon be a young country.

The mere pressure of the children is already transforming the French way of life. At the moment the population rise imposes an especially heavy burden on the French wage earner, for a graph of the present population can be likened to a dumbbell, with many old people at one extreme, very many young people at the other and a comparatively small middle group supporting both the young and the old.

But the burden is well worth bearing. What World War I did not effectively teach, World War II clearly did. A stagnant France was surely doomed to military defeats, to impotence, to dreaming of past glories. Many of the old French habits were condemned by the ordeal of 1940–1945. As a result the old arranged marriages and the carefully limited families are no longer seen as examples of necessary prudence. People marry at a younger age, have bigger families and are less thrifty and less timid. French people travel far more than they used to. France not only imports tourists; she now exports them.

The younger generation is forcing the door open, not just knocking on it. The old closed French family, the old closed French circle of friends is giving way to a pattern of life that is more American than traditionally European. By American standards the older Frenchman is still cagey about making friends, about inviting "strangers" to his house, about discussing his business with anybody but very intimate friends. But the young people—hiking, skiing, driving off in the millions of cheap cars or astride the millions of motor scooters, deeply influenced by the picture of American life given by the movies and American fiction, observing the freer social life of England and Germany—are consciously and unconsciously transforming themselves and their country.

In no modern western country is the gap between generations more obvious than in France —more obvious in dress, speech, amusements and ambitions. This transformation is quickest and most profound in the booming industrial regions that the tourist doesn't see. But it is at work everywhere. In the shadow of great cathedrals or under the walls of great castles, this new modern France is being made.

FRENCH civilization is so old, its roots so deep, national pride (or conceit) so powerful, that there is no real danger of France losing her special "Frenchness." But a France that is young in body and spirit is something that Europe and the world have not seen for a century. No one knows what will come of this change, this rejuvenation. All that one can be sure of is that the new France will be exciting.

Ten years from now the great French tourist attractions, the great French cultural glories will remain the same as always: Paris, the Riviera, Versailles, the cathedrals and the castles. So will the luxury trades and the great vineyards. But they will be inset as ornaments in a new France, more modern, more populous, more rich, more powerful. Maybe she will be a less agreeable country. But that is something for the tourist to wonder about. The young French by that time will have other worries.

YOUNG MOTHER in a Paris park cares for her baby. The parks have been particularly crowded since the recent birth rate rise.

BALL GAME is played in the Tuileries gardens near the Place de la Concorde, a curé's team arrayed against a schoolteacher's team.

Wellspring of Vitality

The French people are known to all mankind for the enthusiasm they bring to the art of living. Their irrepressible *joie de vivre* shows in the happy look of a mother with her baby and in the carefree play of school children in a Paris park. The French ability to laugh at (or with) anyone, combined with an intense feeling for the past, is perhaps a key to the country's energy over the ages and its famous recuperative powers. Expressed in brick and stone, this vitality is enduringly evident in the stern vigor of the great Gothic cathedrals and boundless majesty of Renaissance châteaux, shown on the following pages.

RURAL LIFE *has an unchanging quality. Country people harbor a lively skepticism of new agricultural methods, and in many regions fields are tilled much as they would have been in medieval times*

JOVIAL COUNTENANCE is displayed by the local black-smith of the village of Marsan as he returns from a morning of helping out in the fields, scythe over his shoulder.

EXALTED SETTING exists for this farmer of the Beauce, southwest of Paris, who plows his wheat fields within sight of the stately 13th Century Cathedral of Chartres.

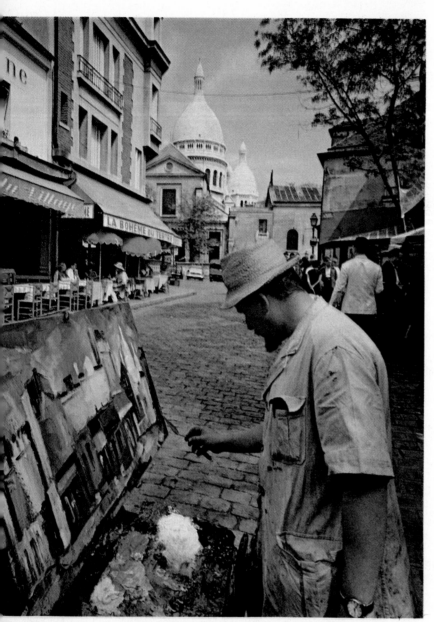

IN MONTMARTRE, perennial mecca of artists, a painter works on a street scene below the white dome of Sacré-Coeur. On Sunday he will very likely try to sell his painting to one of the hundreds of eager tourists who will jam the hilly cobblestone streets and winding alleys of the ancient district and crowd its numerous sidewalk cafés.

AT THE ARC DE TRIOMPHE a young tourist asks a policeman which of the 12 avenues radiating from this focal point of the city she should take. The great arch, one of the most revered of French monuments, was built in the time of Napoleon. Beneath its span burns a continual flame at the tomb of the Unknown Soldier of World War I.

GREAT CHATEAUX, *among the most opulent and magnificent in the world, grace the Loire Valley. Built as pleasure palaces by the kings and noblemen of the 16th and 17th Centuries, they are the finest work of the French Renaissance. In them, ornate rooms provided an elegant setting for court ceremony*

ANTLER TROPHIES of years of hunting hang in a greenhouse at Cheverny, a lavish country house near Blois. Like other châteaux Cheverny has its own hunting park.

KING'S BEDROOM at Cheverny is decorated with eight large tapestries depicting the story of Ulysses, while the ceiling and remaining walls are filled with paintings of scenes from Greek mythology. Even châteaux not owned by the king had specially decorated rooms set aside for the monarch to use when he tired of his own palaces.

ILLUMINATED dramatically at dusk, the sumptuous château of Amboise looms over its venerable town on the Loire. Built in large part by Italian artisans, this château was for a time the home of Leonardo da Vinci. The great round tower at left has a spiral ramp suitable for carriages and cavaliers.

23

FILM CELEBRITIES *have made France's name synonymous with naughty femininity, with droll, down-to-earth humor and with gay, imaginative escapades*

TOP COMEDIAN, Fernandel exemplifies the Man of the South—argumentative, boastful, somewhat ridiculous. Here he offers up a dish of seafood at a Riviera restaurant.

REIGNING ACTRESS, Brigitte Bardot (*opposite*) primps while on film location. Her tousled, pouting "sex kitten" look instigated fads and influenced fashions everywhere.

NONCHALANT HERO, Jean-Paul Belmondo has starred in a series of spectaculars. In *Up to His Ears* he and Ursula Andress survive some antic misadventures in the Far East.

LOST IN PRAYER, an elderly woman stands in fervent concentration as she receives the benediction during a solemn commemorative ritual.

RISING IN BEAUTY, the spidery framework of stone and stained glass in the St.-Denis basilica near Paris is witness to French religious fervor.

FIERY PATRIOT, a Napoleonic grenadier who shouts "Long live the Emperor!" is the subject of a statue by Richefeu in the flag-draped Musée de l'Armée in Paris.

The Weight of a Glorious History

DURING the American Civil War, a young western soldier was found gazing in admiration at Trinity Church in New York. He explained his admiration: in the West, where he had grown to manhood, there was no work of man's hands older than himself.

No French soldier or civilian for many, many centuries past could have known this emotion. Everywhere he goes the Frenchman is in sight of magnificent material achievements, old and not quite so old, that he can at best hope to equal but not to surpass. He will not build a more beautiful church than the Cathedral of Chartres; a more magnificent palace than Versailles; a more elegant square than the Place Stanislas in Nancy; a more impressive memorial than the Arc de Triomphe in Paris. He is in continual competition with the great past.

And that great past is forever being extended backward in time. A dog disappearing into a hole in southern France during World War II led to the discovery of the cave paintings of Lascaux, which are thought to have been done by Cro-Magnon man some 20,000 years ago. The remarkable paintings are a reminder of how long this land of France has been the home of intelligent men. In 1953 a French archaeologist probing a burial mound in Vix, near Châtillon-sur-Seine in eastern France, discovered the tomb of a Celtic princess, which revealed articles showing the cultural sophistication of Gaul 500 years before Christ.

THE French past is very ancient. New discoveries are continually being made, discoveries that show what a high level of artistic achievement these remote ancestors had attained. But the history of what we now call France begins with the wandering Celts, who moved out of central Europe in the Fifth and Fourth Centuries B.C. and spread all over western Europe, raiding as far as Rome (which they burned) and later into the heart of Asia Minor. The greatest center of Celtic settlement was Gaul, a region which was properly bounded by the Rhine River, the Alps and the Pyrenees Mountains, but which also included parts of present-day Switzerland and northern Italy. The land on which the invaders settled was fertile, with a good climate and great natural resources.

Into the land later came Greek traders, and across the Rhine in the Second Century B.C. came Germanic invaders coveting the rich lands occupied by the Gaulish aristocracy. The Greek ports along the Mediterranean like Massilia (Marseilles) passed under Roman control in 121 B.C. So did the territory behind them, which became the first Roman province north of the Alps. To this day it bears the name Provence and is deeply marked by Roman influence. And about 50 years before Christ, Julius Caesar invaded Gallia (Gaul) to restore and improve his political position at home. In the eight years of the Gallic Wars, Caesar defeated the various rival tribes.

In a remarkably short period of time this great and, by Roman standards, empty country was Romanized. The Gallic language disappeared and was replaced by the very imperfect Latin of the Roman soldiers, which in due course developed into what we now call French.

After Christianity was established as a legal religion in the Roman Empire in 313 A.D. the bishops of the Gallic cities became important officials, and it was they who preserved Roman traditions in the dark days of the collapse of the empire in the Fourth and Fifth Centuries. Across the Rhine in these centuries swarmed a series of barbaric invaders—Visigoths, Burgundians, Vandals, Alamans and even the far more remote Huns, headed by their great war chief Attila. The Huns were finally driven back by a combined Gallo-Roman and Visigothic army at the Battle of Châlons in 451, in the Marne River area where so many battles have since been fought. But the final victor was the comparatively obscure tribe of Franks who first had ravaged Gaul in the Third Century. Their chief, Clovis (a name from which we derive Louis), won the political support of the influential Catholic bishops and went on to attain sovereignty over most of Gaul. In 496 he was baptized a Catholic, and during his reign the Franks became the most powerful of the Gallic peoples. What was to be a new nation arose from the merging of the Franks and the Gallo-Romans.

The descendants of Clovis were mostly murderous and idle, and power passed to the "mayors of the palace," who were to the nominal kings what many an American political boss has been to his nominal superior. Eventually the mayors grew tired of the farce and in the Eighth Century they were recognized as kings by the Pope.

IT was already the chief job of the King of the Franks to save what was beginning to be called France from the invaders who came from all sides. The greatest ruler in this period was that King of the Franks whom the French call Charlemagne (Charles the Great). Crowned emperor by the Pope in the year 800, Charlemagne ruled over not only Gaul but almost all of western Germany and most of Italy. He became a legendary figure to both the French and the Germans, but his empire in turn crumbled away, assailed by the Norsemen of Norway and Denmark, who seized the lower valleys of the Seine in the Ninth and 10th Centuries and turned the area into the Duchy of Normandy. Other invaders followed, and all over France castles and strongholds were built on the hills to fend off the repeated incursions. France became a "dark and bloody ground."

IT was around the masters of these isolated castles that the miserable peasants grouped themselves, accepting almost any conditions in return for protection. In the few remaining towns squatting in the ruins of the Roman cities and in the new towns forming in the shelter of abbeys and feudal castles it was the local bishop or great noble who protected if he could. The heirs of Charlemagne—the Carolingian kings—went the way of the heirs of Clovis. Their territory and power gradually dropped away, and in 987 what was left of the nominal authority of the Carolingians passed into the hands of the Count of Paris, Hugh Capet. The founder of the Capetian dynasty, Capet had undisputed control of only a small area of about 3,000 square miles, but as king he theoretically had a domain the size of France today.

The king was not necessarily or often the most powerful ruler in France. But he was sacred because he was anointed at Reims with the oil that had been used to anoint the first Catholic king, Clovis. And only the man so anointed was the rightful ruler of France. Furthermore, Paris, the seat of his power, was at the center of the richest and most fertile part of France. The royal territories were called Ile-de-France (the island of France). Generation after generation under the rule of the Capetians, which extended from the 10th to the 14th Century—a period we know as the Middle Ages—the authority of the king spread.

More important, in seeking ways to overcome the dukes and lesser nobility who were his rivals, the king took for his allies the rising middle classes of the towns. By the middle of the 13th Century the ruler of Paris was the most important king in all Europe, and his capital city was the intellectual glory of the continent. And for nearly all Frenchmen the marriage between the royal family, "the House of France," and what was now called "the French people" was made in heaven—by divine right—and was therefore indissoluble.

This feeling was dramatized in the 14th Century, when the English king invaded France and laid claim to the French throne. During the so-called Hundred Years' War (1337–1453) which ensued, much of France fell under the control of the English. But the mass of the French people were committed to the cause of the legitimate heir, and his cause was sanctified by the support of a surprisingly astute and remarkably heroic girl from the extreme eastern frontier of the kingdom, Jeanne d'Arc, known to the English as Joan of Arc. It was Joan's object not only to "boot the English out of France," as she put it, but to see that the sacred rite of anointing was performed at Reims. This she did, and in 1429 the dauphin, or heir apparent, was crowned Charles VII. In the end Joan was betrayed and burned alive by the English and their French allies. But she had given her countrymen their most sacred legend. And when the Hundred Years' War had ended and the English had been expelled, France was united. The country was ruled from Paris and her boundaries soon became much the same as they are today.

FRANCE now was not only politically united to a far greater degree than any other state on the continent of Europe. She was more and more culturally united. The French spoken in Paris began to spread all over the territories of the King of France. Peasants might speak local dialects, but the nobility, the official classes, the middle class and the clergy learned French and came to use Breton or Catalan or German or Provençal only at home. Whatever their origin, all felt honored by being French.

The 16th Century, however, brought a new kind of division. For the great anti-Catholic rebellion which is known as the Protestant Reformation did not completely conquer France as it did England and Scotland. Nor was it completely stamped out as in Spain or Italy. The French Protestants included various members of the royal family, prominent noblemen, at least one cardinal, a large proportion of the middle classes and much of the peasantry, especially in the South. They fought a series of civil wars to protect themselves and, if possible, to rule France. The great massacre of St. Bartholomew's Eve in 1572 took an estimated 2,000 lives in Paris and at least three times that many in the provinces, but it did not destroy the Protestant party. It merely infuriated it. Peace came when the Protestant king, Henry IV, decided that Paris was "worth a mass"—*i.e.*, he would renounce Protestantism and become a Catholic in order to placate the Catholics and secure his throne. Henry also issued the Edict of Nantes (1598), guaranteeing religious toleration—indeed, religious favors—to his former fellow Protestants.

France thereupon saw a period of relative religious peace, but the memories of the religious wars died hard and when Louis XIV in 1685 revoked the toleration that his grandfather Henry IV had guaranteed, he reopened a wound which has not yet healed. As a result of the revocation many hundreds of thousands of "Huguenots," the name then popularly given to French Protestants, fled to London, to Amsterdam—and to towns in America like New Rochelle outside New York. And hundreds of thousands of embittered Huguenots remained in France.

UNDER Louis XIV (1643–1715) the splendor of the monarch and of the French people reached its height. Louis was called "the Sun King": all power and enlightenment radiated from him. His palace at Versailles was the most magnificent in Europe. With France setting the standards for the civilized world, the French language became *the* second language of all educated men everywhere and the first language of many. The academies of Berlin, St. Petersburg and Stockholm were modeled after the French Academy. Even after the power of the French state had declined in later centuries, the cultural predominance of France remained unchallenged. No subsequent writer has known the universal glory of the great 18th Century philosopher and wit, Voltaire.

The illustrious Louis XIV, after a successful war, had adopted the motto *Nec pluribus impar* ("a match for many"). But his arrogance made the many more. His expulsion of the Huguenots rallied Protestant Europe—England, Holland and the German princes—against him, and the French army suffered a series of defeats, most notably at the Battle of Blenheim in 1704. It was the end of an era.

ALL through the 18th Century the power of the French state declined. France grew richer; the King of France grew poorer. India was lost to England; so was Canada. True, King Louis XVI (1774–1792) took his revenge on England by successfully helping the rebelling American colonies to gain their independence. But this effort finally bankrupted his treasury, and the French Revolution began.

No one foresaw in 1789 that the reorganization of France, which nearly everyone agreed was necessary because of the country's outdated political and economic system and the monarchy's inability to bring about the necessary reforms, would take the violent and decisive form it did. Less than four years after Louis XVI had called on the representatives of his people —the Estates-General—for advice and money, these representatives had declared France a republic and the king had been executed. France was not only a republic but one that cut itself off from the past and promised a new political and social order to Europe and to America. Every aspect of French life was examined, amended or condemned. The revolutionaries even adopted a brand-new calendar and dated history from 1792, "Year One of the Republic."

The Revolution abolished the divine right of kings and replaced it with a political authority based on the will of the people. Every institution in France had to justify itself, nominally if not in fact, on the basis of popular decision. The recent American example of democratic independence was very potent in creating a climate of opinion in which the reorganization of France on a democratic basis was both possible and necessary. But the differences between the American and French Revolutions were as significant as the resemblances. Federalism, the basis of the new American system, was considered reactionary in France. More important still, the Constitution which was drawn up following the American Revolution settled the problem of political authority in the United States so that it was only once put in question, in the Civil War; the French Revolution, on the other hand, asked the question of authority but did not answer it effectively.

The French Revolution, in fact, degenerated into a very bloody civil war and was the parent of later domestic revolts. Thousands of Frenchmen were driven into exile. Thousands were massacred. Thousands died by the new humanitarian method of execution, the guillotine. Between the old France and the new a deep ditch was dug and filled with blood.

Meanwhile, disagreements within the country, coupled with the messianic fervor of the revolutionary government, led to wars between France and her neighbors. France was invaded in 1792, and only by enormous effort did she repel the intruders.

IN an optimistic effort to heal some of the wounds the Revolution had inflicted, the government in 1795 changed the name of the great square in Paris where the guillotine had stood from the Place de la Révolution to the Place de la Concorde. But it was easier to decree concord than to secure it. And the great war still continued. Now, however, France was not being invaded but was invading her neighbors, and French armies were carrying everywhere the revolutionary doctrine and practice.

There were violent partisans of the French republic in Dublin and Edinburgh, in Vienna and Amsterdam. Wordsworth, Coleridge, Kant, Beethoven and Jefferson had welcomed the new

RULERS AND GOVERNMENTS

MEROVINGIANS

481-511	Clovis, first French king
511-751	Descendants of Clovis

CAROLINGIANS

751-768	Pepin the Short
768-814	Charlemagne, son of Pepin
814-987	Charlemagne's descendants

CAPETIANS

987-996	Hugh Capet
996-1031	Robert II, the Pious
1031-1060	Henry I
1060-1108	Philip I
1108-1137	Louis VI, the Fat
1137-1180	Louis VII
1180-1223	Philip II, Augustus
1223-1226	Louis VIII
1226-1270	Louis IX (St. Louis)
1270-1285	Philip III, the Rash
1285-1314	Philip IV
1314-1316	Louis X
1316-1322	Philip V
1322-1328	Charles IV

VALOIS Branch of Capetian Dynasty

1328-1350	Philip VI
1350-1364	John
1364-1380	Charles V
1380-1422	Charles VI
1422-1461	Charles VII
1461-1483	Louis XI
1483-1498	Charles VIII
1498-1515	Louis XII
1515-1547	Francis I
1547-1559	Henry II
1559-1560	Francis II
1560-1574	Charles IX
1574-1589	Henry III

BOURBONS

1589-1610	Henry IV
1610-1643	Louis XIII
1643-1715	Louis XIV
1715-1774	Louis XV
1774-1792	Louis XVI

GOVERNMENTS SINCE THE REVOLUTION

1792-1799	First Republic
1799-1804	Consulate under Napoleon
1804-1814	First Empire—Napoleon Emperor
1814-1824	Louis XVIII—the Bourbon Restoration
1824-1830	Charles X
1830-1848	Louis Philippe I (the July Monarchy)
1848-1852	Second Republic, Louis Napoleon, President
1852-1870	Second Empire, Louis Napoleon becomes Napoleon III
1870-1940	Third Republic
1940-1944	"French State" under Pétain
1944-1946	Provisional Government under De Gaulle
1946-1958	Fourth Republic
1958-	Fifth Republic

PROCESSION OF DYNASTIES is shown in the chart above. Merovingian kings after Clovis and Carolingians after Charlemagne are here omitted as they are unimportant.

world. And then came Napoleon Bonaparte, a new and dynamic leader who took control of France and radically changed the character of the revolutionary movement.

The foreign partisans of the Revolution did not all keep their enthusiasm for it after Napoleon established his dictatorship and turned the republic into an empire in 1804. Napoleon had been the most brilliant of the young generals commanding the republican armies and was a man of the most dazzling and extravagant genius. He continued the great war, but France was now less a liberator than a mere conqueror. In 1812 there were French armies simultaneously in Madrid and Moscow. Rome, Amsterdam and Hamburg were officially parts of France. No nation had ever had such a surfeit of glory.

It was not merely military glory. The new French legal system, the Code Napoléon, was widely admired and copied. The French helped destroy feudal remnants all over western and parts of central Europe. But in less than two years, from the late fall of 1812 to the spring of 1814, the whole structure crashed. Napoleon's Grande Armée straggled back from Moscow and for the first time Russia stepped onto the center of the European stage. Cossacks camped in the heart of Paris. Napoleon was defeated, attempted a comeback and was finally destroyed in 1815 at the Battle of Waterloo.

BUT the memory was not destroyed. For the French bourgeois or peasant, the Revolution was a great and good thing that had found him an underprivileged subject and had made him a man and a citizen. The old unconditional loyalty to the king by divine right was supplanted by the new idea of loyalty to the "nation."

But what nation? The Revolution had divided France again, more deeply than ever before; there had been too much blood on each side for the parties to be reconciled in a common loyalty, despite the introduction in 1814 of a limited monarchy. And there was the intoxicating memory of the brilliant, too brilliant past. As long as the memory of the two million lives lost in the 23 years of the revolutionary and

Napoleonic wars was acute, as long as the memory of the invasions of 1814 and 1815 was lively, the French people were tranquil if not content. But the poison of glory was still running in the national veins. The great roll of battles resounded. Napoleon was now remembered more as a hero than as a dictator. The country's basic political instability was reflected in a procession of short-lived regimes during the 19th Century, including a Second Empire between 1852 and 1870 under Napoleon's nephew, Napoleon III. And there were wars—minor wars, but savage and bloody wars all the same. The conquest of Algeria, which began in 1830, lasted almost 20 years and cost many thousands of lives. There were wars in Italy and the Crimea and even in Mexico.

THEN calamity struck, in the form of the Franco-Prussian War. In 1870 France blundered into fighting the newly uniting German states and was decisively beaten. And after Paris had succumbed to the invaders, the Paris workers and craftsmen rose against the new conservative French government. The revolt was put down savagely in 1871: far more damage was done to Paris by the French than by the Germans. The monument is there, the great gap in the Tuileries gardens where children play today. There stood the great Tuileries palace of the French kings that was burned by the despairing rebels in the last days of the Commune. And a greater loss still was that class antagonisms were heightened and fresh memories of violence implanted in the savagery of civil war and in the ruthlessness of repression.

The Commune of Paris has a legendary history better known than its real history. It was in large part a revolt of patriotic Paris workers, small craftsmen and shopkeepers against the surrender of Paris to the Germans. But it was claimed by Karl Marx in London as a Communist uprising. Not very many people in Paris had ever heard of Marx, but the claim, reiterated again and again by Marx and later by Lenin and by their latter-day French disciples, has overlaid the incontrovertible truth that the Commune was a purely French and pre-Socialist uprising.

The defeat of 1870–1871 ended the long reign of "The Great Nation." It soon became apparent that the German victory was no accident. Every kind of power—military, political, economic, above all industrial—was now concentrated on the other side of the Rhine. And, far more terrible, in the peace treaty which followed the war the deeply French eastern provinces of Alsace and Lorraine were torn, against their bitter protests, from the France which, even in defeat, they so greatly preferred to the new and victorious Germany.

The shocks of 1870–1871 were a turning point in French history because, up to this time—despite disasters like the early English invasions, despite the savage wars of religion, despite the horrors of the Revolution, despite the defeats in which the Napoleonic adventure ended—the story of France had been a success story. After 1871, it was not. The acquiring of a large overseas empire during this period did not alter the course of decline.

WITH the outbreak of World War I in 1914, France's chance for revenge came, and in time victory over Germany came too. But victory was possible only because the power of Britain and then that of the United States were thrown into the balance. The cost was desperate. Nearly as many Frenchmen died in battle as the total population of the recovered Alsace-Lorraine. The war was fought in the richest, most modern part of France. Steel mills, coal mines, textile plants, the most fertile soil as well as great monuments like Reims Cathedral were wrecked or shattered in the four-year ordeal.

And to what end? The allies of France withdrew from the support of the peace settlement they had made. The preponderance of Germany was greater than ever, for she had suffered much less than France. Only by insisting on the controversial terms of the Versailles treaty of 1919 and by entering into alliances with the new nations that had sprung from the ruins of the Russian and Austro-Hungarian Empires could the French contrive to neutralize German superiority. All enlightened opinion in Britain and the United States sneered at the foolish fears of the French and pressed for equality for Germany—which meant eventual superiority.

THE French knew and feared their formidable neighbor. Yet in the face of the rise of Adolf Hitler in the 1930s the successive governments of France were paralyzed. Hitler struck when France was weakest. In 1939 the double losses of World War I—the men killed, the boys unborn—both reduced the number of young soldiers to an all-time low and made the thought of another war intolerable to a degree that weakened the country's will to fight for another victory that might be ruinous. The German army's 1940 blitzkrieg broke France in only six weeks.

This was the greatest disaster in French history since the time of Joan of Arc. But the situation was more complicated even than it had been in the 15th Century. For the great hero of World War I, Marshal Henri Philippe Pétain, the victor of Verdun, accepted from the demoralized French parliament the task of salvaging what could be saved for a France held firmly in the grip of a victorious Hitler. At the same time, from London, an obscure general of original views named Charles de Gaulle, a former protégé of Marshal Pétain, issued a call to resistance. "France has lost a battle," he said. "But France has not lost the war."

Who really represented France? It is certain that in the despairing summer of 1940 most Frenchmen supported Pétain, who indeed was recognized as the legitimate ruler of France by the United States. But when it became apparent that Great Britain had not been knocked out, when it became known that the United States was extending aid to Britain, and when Germany's invasion of Russia changed the confused pacifist and collaborationist policy of the French Communist party overnight, more and more Frenchmen joined the Resistance. But the necessity of making the choice divided parents and children, set family against family and introduced new feuds into village life. There were reprisals and counter-reprisals, executions and assassinations, and in their savagery the Nazis were occasionally rivaled by Frenchmen.

By its acceptance of Pétain and of the armistice in June and July of 1940 the Third Republic, born in the 1871 defeat, had committed suicide. Marshal Pétain had even abolished the name Republic. He was the head of the "French State." But this new political organization was itself condemned by the Allied victory. In that victory, France was supposedly a sharer, but in reality she was, like Germany, a defeated nation. The nominal head of the French State, Pétain, was imprisoned for life. The real head, Pierre Laval, was executed. A provisional government was set up, presided over by De Gaulle from 1944 to 1946; in 1946 De Gaulle resigned "irrevocably" and the Fourth Republic came into being. But the country was impoverished. It was a country of whose future many inside and outside France despaired.

MOST Frenchmen did not despair. The postwar economic boom and the baby boom are proof enough of that. But some illusions took a long time to die. There was, for example, the illusion of "a nation of 100 million Frenchmen." This figure had been conjured up before World War II by the simple process of adding the population of France's empire to the population of France and by assuming that everyone in the empire was on his way to becoming a Frenchman. But the "French Union," a proposed federation of all French territories urged by General de Gaulle during the war and formally established in 1946, was never really a going concern politically. The richest of the colonies, Indochina, had to be abandoned in 1954 after a long and costly war. Then it became evident that even in the colonies which did not actively revolt, the inhabitants did not want to become Frenchmen, but wished to develop their own national identities.

In 1958 the Fourth Republic, plagued by troubles both at home and overseas—particularly in Algeria (*see Chapter 3*)—collapsed. De Gaulle returned to power and organized the Fifth Republic. The French Union gave way

that year to the French Community, but the elaborate institutions set up for it had a short life, for, with the exception of a few islands, all the members of the Community chose independence. Nearly all chose it in a spirit of friendliness to France and began negotiating treaties of mutual support with their former rulers. But the dream of empire was over.

THE French learned another lesson. They had to come to terms with Germany. Oddly enough, there was less anti-German feeling in France after World War II than after World War I, even though this time the Germans had behaved much worse. The change may have been made possible by a transfer of guilt from "the Germans" to "the Nazis." It was also made easier by the fact that a great deal of French anger was expended on Frenchmen who had collaborated with the Germans.

But there was a deeper feeling among many Frenchmen—though there was opposition as well—that only in a Franco-German partnership could either country feel secure. Beyond Germany lay a Russia frighteningly strong. And it was believed that this time a Germany which had suffered so much had learned its lesson. On this foundation De Gaulle was able to impress his personality on the German as well as the French people, to make Chancellor Adenauer a close ally and to bring about a Franco-German political and economic integration that would have seemed incredible as late as 1950.

After World War I the poet Paul Valéry had called Europe "a little cape of the Asiatic continent." It could be no more than that unless it found some unity. And in view of that, what did the old feuds mean? Most Frenchmen today are willing to discard the load of past glory and hate and to ask, as Shelley did in 1821:

> *Oh, cease! must hate and death return?*
> *Cease! must men kill and die?*
> *Cease! drain not to its dregs the urn*
> *Of bitter prophecy.*
> *The world is weary of the past.*
> *Oh, might it die or rest at last!*

Silent testimony to ancient Roman power in Provence, four stately Corinthian columns stand in lonely splendor in a pasture near Riez.

Vestiges of a Grand Past

A cultural crossroads for Europe and one of its principal battlegrounds as well, France is surfeited with magnificent memorials of past ages. Classical ruins in Provence, a quiet region near the Mediterranean Sea, evoke the brilliance of Roman civilization. Medieval cathedrals and Renaissance châteaux recall the country's greatest cultural and monarchial glory. In recent centuries France has chosen to memorialize the heroism of her soldiers during military triumph and tragedy, as if to try to recapture the intoxicating but now vanished feeling of primacy in the world.

37

MONUMENTS TO FAITH, *the graceful Gothic churches*
of France testify to the spirituality of medieval life. Among the most
magnificent of all is the Cathedral of St. Stephen at Bourges

AT DUSK the Bourges Cathedral projects against the sky like a gilded crown. Built in the 13th Century, the church is partly bounded by a formal grove. Unlike most cathedrals it has no transept (cross aisle) but its stained glass (*left*) is among the finest in the world.

39

HERO'S TOMB, the gigantic sarcophagus of Napoleon (*opposite*) lies in public view in the Paris monument called the Dôme des Invalides. This picture was taken from the floor to show the high, wide dome.

NATION'S LOSS is commemorated at the military cemetery at Verdun, where more than 350,000 French soldiers died during World War I. At right a peg-legged caretaker gets ready to raise the French tricolor.

AN END TO OVERSEAS EMPIRE *came in the 1950s as French administrators and French troops withdrew from territorial possessions in Asia and Africa after 400 years of colonial rule*

LOWERING THE TRICOLOR at Hanoi in October 1954, French soldiers prepare to leave Indochina after eight years of warfare which cost France 147,000 casualties.

AN ALGERIAN WELCOME is given to Charles de Gaulle as he tours the capital city of Algiers in June 1958. The unpopularity of the Algerian war caused the downfall of the Fourth Republic and brought him back into power. Six months later, De Gaulle was the Fifth Republic's first president and Algeria was on the way to independence.

In one of the many disturbances that have plagued French politics for generations, left-wing demonstrators protest against the government

The Politics of Instability

rmistice Day ceremonies in 1948 by organizing a mass march down the Champs Elysées and angrily hurling café chairs at the police.

IN 1789, the year when the Constitution of the United States went into effect, the French people set about giving themselves a liberal constitution to replace the tottering system of absolute monarchy. The United States today is still governed under the constitution it adopted in 1789, but the current French constitution, overwhelmingly approved by popular vote in 1958, represents the 13th attempt to give stable political institutions to France.

The institutions of the Fifth Republic were quite like those of the Third and Fourth. They included, for example, a president of the Republic and a Senate, both indirectly elected. But General de Gaulle has transformed his own constitution by making the office of president far more important than the constitutional text justifies and by changing the method of election of the president to a direct vote. There is no reason to believe that these changes have caused any deep resentment; nevertheless the very fact that it has been so easy to transform a constitution solemnly adopted in 1958 has increased natural French skepticism about the stability of

GOSHEN COLLEGE LIBRARY
GOSHEN, INDIANA

political institutions. But politics is not everything, for governing is also a matter of civil administration. Here France has not been unstable. Perhaps she has even been too stable.

Much of the old monarchial administrative system survived the Revolution of 1789. There had been—and still is—a competent and honest body of civil servants directed from Paris. Government in France has had great continuity as well as repeated change, and the average Frenchman, outside Paris at least, has been less conscious of violent change in the public matters that concern him than of a slower, more evolutionary and far less dramatic adaptation of venerable institutions to modern needs. The adaptation may not have been fast enough or thorough enough, but it has been constant and its results have been permanent.

THE reforms of the Revolution divided the country into departments, arrondissements, cantons and communes. The arrondissements and cantons have little importance today, but the departments and communes matter a great deal. In the 95 departments (roughly comparable in size to large American counties) and in the 38,-000 communes (which range from tiny villages to great cities) lies the effective power of local self-government in France.

The organization of local government under the Revolution was given a backbone by the administrative changes of Napoleon, above all by the creation of the office of prefect, an agent of the central government with duties and powers unparalleled in America. He has in theory—and largely in practice—a complete right of supervision of all local government bodies in his department. His duty is to see that the orders of the central government are carried out and also that the elected local bodies do not exceed their powers. If the local councils do not do what they should, or if they do what they should not, the prefect or his subordinates can take the necessary steps to set matters aright.

On paper this seems like a recipe for great prefectural power, because local government in France is like self-government in a college or a

jail: it is limited to what the superior powers will permit. But the important political fact is that the local councils that are thus limited are elected by popular vote. Furthermore, the voters who choose the members of the councils also elect the French National Assembly. And most of the representatives who are directly elected by the people to the Assembly are also members of these local bodies, and usually they are the leaders of the councils. So are the men who are chosen indirectly (by the local councilors among others) for the Senate. This fact alone limits the power of the prefects and determines the character of French local government.

Why? Because every prefect is appointed on the understanding that he will not cause unnecessary trouble for the central government. "No incidents, please," is the assumed instruction. And the popularly elected councilors with whom the prefect has to deal in the communes and departments are almost always people with deep roots. Although the French are alleged (with some justice) to be ungrateful to national politicians, they are extremely faithful to their local leaders. The late Premier Edouard Herriot, for example, who was one of the most popular politicians of modern French history, experienced many ups and downs during his long political career in Paris, but he was also mayor of Lyons for almost 50 years and he died in that office. All over France, the local leaders are men whose personal power is so great that only a very foolish prefect would willingly and without good reason tangle with them. The fundamental stability of France and the country's legendary recuperative powers can be understood only if this grass-roots democracy is taken into account.

THESE local leaders are often active leaders in the national political parties. But their strength is more a matter of personality than of party position. There is not much chance for "carpetbaggers" or outsiders. Some local leaders are doctors, more are lawyers—not only trial lawyers but men who look after wills, transfers of property, tax questions and other matters of local importance. Others are small businessmen. A small village may elect the only man who has a college education. Or it may even elect the biggest farmer or the local nobleman.

In one area of rural France, for example, there was a nobleman who, like his father and grandfather before him, had been mayor of the village where his more remote ancestors were once feudal lords. But the noble mayor (who had once been an ambassador) had a useless and idle son. So he was succeeded on his death (not before) by his assistant mayor—the local blacksmith, a Communist.

Such personal considerations, of course, do not obtain as much in the big cities. There party labels do matter. But even in the cities, personality counts for quite a lot. Performance, personality and probity (French *local* government is usually very honest) add strength to the party ticket, and in many cases the party owes more to its local representatives than they owe to it. On the local level the voters don't want a party administration; they want a regime that meets their own needs acceptably. Here lie the permanent and indestructible foundations of French democracy. It was not accidental that although the French people in the 1958 referendum voted almost 80 per cent for General de Gaulle's constitution, the same voters a few months later quickly re-elected to the various local councils their old familiar leaders whether these men were Gaullists or not.

IT is not hard to see why there has been such strong loyalty to local leaders. Revolution, war, invasion and occupation have overthrown national institutions and sent into exile, obscurity or even to death many national leaders. But the local politicians all the while have been doing local jobs, including the job of protecting the department, city or village against "outsiders" in Paris.

Those politicians who have jobs both locally and in the central government are aware that they must keep their local base secure. They must come down constantly from Paris to sit with the local council or to hold a kind of court

in the town hall. Their aim is not merely to dispense favors but to test public opinion on a score of locally important matters, from the condition of the streets to the possible building of a sports stadium.

It is in the villages that the strength of local government is most visible. The village mayor is not usually a representative in Paris as well, so he is on the job all the time. His voters accost him in the streets and they invade his home or his little office, which is often in the schoolhouse building. They pester his secretary, who frequently is also the village schoolmaster. They want to have explained to them the unintelligible orders from the prefect that have been posted up on the village notice board. They want advice on how to obey some regulation, or how to disobey it and get away with it.

So we see the mayor alone, or with his councilors, going about his business while the sounds and smells of the farmyards give a special flavor to the laborious and thrifty consideration of village affairs. It is a real world in which a phony cannot long survive and in which, when you get a good man, you keep him in for life. Here is government within reach of everybody.

DESPITE all these assets, however, most Frenchmen since World War I have come to expect more from their local government than thrift, honesty and a few minimum services. Some of the success that Communists have enjoyed in local elections has been deserved. The Communists were pioneers in providing more than just clean streets and efficient street lighting. They have furnished (at the taxpayers' expense) children's playgrounds, day nurseries, municipal swimming pools, public housing and public entertainment. Sometimes, admittedly, their efforts have taken comic forms. In one mountain village a victorious Communist council built a lavish underground comfort station in the public square. If many of the inhabitants were puzzled, it was because the community was one in which indoor toilets of any kind were a rarity.

But the Communists were not the only ones to insist that local government do more. The

Frenchwoman did not get the vote until after World War II. But when she did, she wanted more than the male voter did. She wanted clinics, more parks and children's playgrounds, and more medical facilities for mothers, even if it meant raising the tax rate. Now the new ideas of what can and should be done locally are deeply rooted, even among men.

The chief barrier to expansion of local power in France is not the veto of the prefect or of the other central agents, but money. French cities and towns have very inelastic sources of revenue. Dependent largely on grants from the central government, they can add little to their basic income. They can tax lap dogs at a higher rate than sheep dogs (which in the country are not a luxury), and they can collect license fees from business activities. But what in America is called "municipal home rule" is unknown in France. Local law-enforcement power is also limited. In every commune with a population above 10,000, police powers are largely in the hands of the central government, which has in addition the nationwide *gendarmerie* as a weapon to repress crime and maintain order. Since 1947 the government has also had at its disposal a number of highly mobile and very tough "special companies" created specifically to deal with rioting by Communists and others. They were meant to be "tough cops," and they are.

WHEN we turn from local to national politics we are not turning to a totally different world. There is an endless web woven between the two. Success in winning control of local councils pays off nationally. Control of municipalities, which present opportunities for political patronage, has strengthened the power of such eminent party leaders as Guy Mollet of the Socialists. And at another level, a successful local administrator, Jacques Chaban-Delmas, who has been elected and re-elected mayor of Bordeaux since 1947, wields even greater influence in national politics as the capable Gaullist speaker of the National Assembly.

Nevertheless, if national and local politics are intertwined, they are very different in tone

and effectiveness. Under the Third and Fourth Republics, from 1870 to 1958, effective power was in the hands of the national parliament, and this power was jealously preserved. A crisis might put a strong man in office as premier, but the average member of parliament was always waiting for the time when the strong executive would no longer be necessary and could be gotten rid of. Premiers were in daily, even hourly danger of being overthrown by a hostile vote. They had to spend more time preparing for and dodging parliamentary ambushes than planning or carrying out long-term policies.

SOME of the most important achievements of the Third and Fourth Republics—the vast expansion of France's colonial empire in the first instance, the Monnet Plan in the second (*see Chapter 4*)—were carried to success with only intermittent parliamentary authority. Parliament was above all a negative power, quicker to destroy than to create. And it was an arena where the numerous traditional and present-day quarrels dividing Frenchmen were continually fought over. The contrast with local government was striking, although it should be remembered that by elevating most controversial questions (like control of the schools) to the national level the central government made comparative peace easier to attain locally—and harder to attain nationally.

But even if the parliament did not do much to reduce internal divisions, it did not invent them. In a sense, French parliamentary government was too representative. France *was* divided, and the parliament reflected this fact. There were regional divisions between town and country and between North and South. There were religious divisions between Catholics and Protestants in some areas and—more commonly—between the partisans of the Catholic Church and its secular opponents. There were class divisions dating from early workers' rebellions, and there were other divisions arising from the confused and bitter years of World War II.

Finally, the instability of the French central government has made automatic loyalty to that government very difficult. A Frenchman born 50 years ago has had to live under four different governmental systems. France's greatest contemporary hero, General de Gaulle, was sentenced to death during World War II as a rebel by the government of Marshal Pétain; after the war, Pétain in turn was tried and imprisoned for life as a traitor.

A Frenchman looking at the government of the day naturally keeps his fingers crossed. He may want passionately to serve his country, but that is not the same thing as believing passionately in the rightful authority of the particular persons in office to represent the nation. Since 1958 the French have had stability under President de Gaulle. But the 1965 elections, in which De Gaulle failed to win a majority on the first ballot and had to campaign in a runoff contest, reaffirmed a traditional French reluctance to give their leaders unconditional allegiance or unlimited power. Only in a rare crisis is the average Frenchman willing to support his government with anything like absolute trust and obedience. Many of the troubles of France come from unstable political institutions, though more come from the bitterly divided history of France.

WHATEVER the reasons were, the troubled history of the Fourth Republic convinced an increasing proportion of Frenchmen (and Frenchwomen) that political institutions had a good deal to do with French failures, for instance with the failure either to win the war in Indochina in 1954 or to end it earlier and in a less disastrous fashion. The aims and the methods of the politicians in the National Assembly in Paris seemed to have little to do with the fears and hopes and needs of the voters. The façade of the building in which the National Assembly met had no windows, and many Frenchmen thought this was symbolic: the politicians were looking inward instead of outward. For reasons that the public thought were purely self-seeking, the "government"—the premier and his cabinet—fell on an average of every six months. Continuity of policy was impossible. Difficult problems were postponed rather than solved, and

pressure groups were outrageously powerful. An increasing part of the voting population was alienated from the "system."

By May, 1958, public patience was coming to an end. It was the outbreak of rioting among the French population of Algiers, supported by disgruntled army officers, that destroyed the Fourth Republic and brought General de Gaulle back to power. Even if this crisis had not taken place, the Fourth Republic, incapable of solving urgent problems and not getting credit for those it did solve, might have collapsed anyway.

WHEN De Gaulle came into power in 1958 he could undoubtedly have proposed any type of constitution and had it accepted. Both he and the nation wanted a governmental system that would avoid the weaknesses of the Fourth Republic; indeed, the Constitution of the Fifth Republic is best understood as a conscious rejection of the governmental practices of the Fourth. First of all, the executive branch has been given far more extensive powers than it had under the old system. The "government" has been given control of the business of the parliament; now it is the government's program that is voted on, not the program proposed by the standing committees of the Assembly.

Although the government still has to have the "confidence" of the Assembly, that confidence is now harder to withdraw. To overthrow a government it is now necessary to obtain an absolute majority of the Assembly. The president, after consulting the premier and the presidents of the two parliamentary houses, can declare the dissolution of the National Assembly after its first year of life and thus appeal directly to the voters against their nominal representatives. The constitution also undercuts the old temptation on the part of the deputies to overthrow a government merely in order to participate in the new government that would have to be formed, for now a deputy who becomes a cabinet minister must resign his seat in the Assembly.

The new Senate or upper house now wields far more power than it was allowed under the

Fourth Republic. Indeed, it has almost the same powers as the Assembly, and if the government so chooses it can ally itself with the Senate to block legislation the Assembly wants; or on the other hand it can combine with the Assembly to overrule the Senate.

ALTHOUGH De Gaulle was known to admire the American system of government more than the English, the new constitution was drawn up with the intention of giving France a variation on the English type of cabinet government, not a variant on the American type of presidential government. In effect, however, the office of president of the Republic has entirely eclipsed that of premier. If De Gaulle had preferred to be premier, that office would have had the importance that the constitutional text provided for. But he preferred to be president, and, to amend an old saying, "Wherever De Gaulle sits is the head of the table." Under the 1958 constitution the effective head of the French executive is the president, not the premier, and France today has a governmental system much more like that of the United States than that of Britain.

Given the great prestige of General de Gaulle, it perhaps could not have been otherwise. But there is more than the weight of his personality behind the fact that the new constitution has not worked according to plan. The attempt to imitate English cabinet government would in any case have foundered on the French multiparty system. On the conservative side, there have been hardly any real parties. Traditionally, most conservatives have grouped themselves into very loose blocs held together chiefly by sentiment and interest, and important mainly because of their local strength. Each "party" has gotten its power from its nominees; it has had none of its own to give them in return. The center parties have been grouped around personalities with a wider appeal, but again the party as such has been less important than its parliamentary representatives.

A few parties, particularly those on the Left, have had organized support and some internal discipline. But there has been no possibility of forming a government out of one party. For France to have a two-party system, France would have to have had a different history. And without a two-party system, parliamentary government on the English model was impossible under the Third and Fourth Republics, and it would also have been impossible under the Fifth, if the experiment had been tried.

The experiment has not been tried. The personal prestige of General de Gaulle has been so great that the U.N.R. (Union for the New Republic), whose only reason for existence is General de Gaulle, has with its allies had a majority in the Assembly. But it could be said that the only disciplined *party* in French politics is the Communist party. This disagreeable fact has helped to weaken French democracy and to destroy governmental efficiency since the end of World War II.

Normally about a fifth of the French electorate votes the Communist ticket. True, in the referendum of 1958 more than a million people who normally vote Communist must have voted for General de Gaulle. But when the time came a few months later to vote for the local councilors, who form the bulk of the electoral college that chooses the Senate, they went back, in the main, to their old loyalty.

TO be sure, the strength of the Communist party is grossly exaggerated if we look only at the votes cast for its candidates. Party members constitute less than a tenth of the Communist voting strength and only a small proportion of the members make up the militant "hard core." But the success of the Communists in getting such a large number of votes has made the working of parliamentary government in France even more difficult than it was already. Ever since the Socialists broke with the Communists in 1947, the Communists have been effectively disbarred from playing a normal role in politics. No party, aside from a tiny fellow-traveling group, has been willing to ally itself openly or tacitly with the Communists to form a government. (François Mitterand, in the 1965 presidential election, accepted Communist support, but claimed he had made no promises.)

Why do millions of French voters continue to vote for Communists? The explanation can be found, as so often in France, in history. It is the history of legend and of myth. The legend for a century has been that the French worker has been cheated. And the legend is not totally devoid of truth. The town or city worker, above all the Paris worker, was the maker of the Revolution. And he got less out of it, if he obtained anything at all, than did the middle-class shopkeeper, the small manufacturer, the lawyer or the doctor—and a lot less than the members of the upper middle class, who profited both socially and economically. The worker also got less than the peasant, though in modern times the poor peasant, especially in the backward regions of the French countryside, has himself been less and less content with what he won from the Revolution. The legend is that the worker, and the peasant as well, has been robbed. To end the robbery, the rules must be changed. The Revolution must continue.

THE necessary myth was produced by the Russian Revolution, which had reportedly established a worker's paradise. Lending added potency to this encouraging myth was the disillusion, felt all over the western world, at the results of World War I. The backwardness of French industry and the meagerness of French social services further soured the worker. He did, in fact, gain a little from the slow modernization of France, but not enough to kill the appeal of the legend or the myth. So in 1920 the majority of the French Socialist party accepted Communist leadership, which meant Russian leadership, and more and more the politically active elements among the workers, and in some regions among the peasants, voted the Communist ticket. A small proportion of them became disciplined members of the party.

The party attempted to create a complete world for the loyal member, and to an alarming extent it succeeded. There were party schools of indoctrination, party newspapers (including the

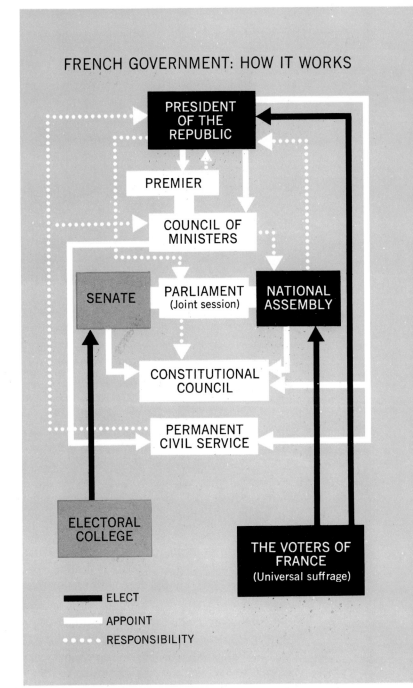

FRENCH GOVERNMENT: HOW IT WORKS

ELECT
APPOINT
RESPONSIBILITY

THE CENTRAL GOVERNMENT now gives greater representation to urban areas than previously, following a 1962 constitutional amendment providing for direct popular election of the president. A largely rural electoral college still elects the Senate. The president has the power to dissolve the Assembly; the Assembly can oust the Council of Ministers and the premier. The Constitutional Council interprets the constitution. The civil service advises the ministers and audits their ministry budgets.

famous onetime-Socialist paper *L'Humanité*), and journals like the peasant-oriented *La Terre* (The Land) directed to special groups. There were athletic clubs, literary clubs and youth groups. There were fighting organizations, both open and secret. The good party member lived in a kind of communal iron lung.

The party insisted on, and obtained, a degree of discipline from the members it sent to the parliament that no other party aimed at, much less achieved. The Communist deputy turned his salary over to the party and received part of it back to live on. If he did not change his voting according to switches in the party line, he was— as far as the party could manage it—ruined.

Russia's signing of a nonaggression pact with Hitler in 1939 threatened for a while to destroy the French Communist organization, for on orders from Moscow the party line was abruptly changed. Instead of advocating an all-out war against Hitler, the party suddenly wanted peace. But Germany's invasion of Russia changed the line back again and saved the party. During the war the Communists provided many of the most heroic and capable members of the Resistance. When liberation came General de Gaulle prevented the Communists from taking cabinet posts controlling the army, the police and the foreign ministry, but they had earned a prestige that took years to become tarnished.

YET the Communist party today is not what it was. It is aging. It recruits fewer and fewer young people. Its appeal to the intellectuals suffered terribly from the Soviet crushing of the Hungarian rebellion. That bloody crime alienated the most famous of French sympathizers, the philosopher Jean-Paul Sartre, and is believed even to have shaken the faith of the artist Pablo Picasso. The Communist-controlled trade union federation has been steadily losing members. The fact that so many Communist voters defied party orders by voting for General de Gaulle's constitution was a blow to the leadership. There is no longer the old faith that France can be made to go the way Czechoslovakia did in 1948. Also, the party is besieged by the intruding

"Americanized" world; the edge of revolutionary zeal is blunted by material well-being.

The same forces have weakened the old Socialist party even more disastrously. It is now split in two. Membership in the more conservative parent party—led by Guy Mollet—is not only declining but aging, and party attempts to build up a powerful trade union federation have been a failure. What mass support there is comes largely from white collar workers. An offshoot party, the Unified Socialists, has as its most eminent member the most dynamic French leader of the Fourth Republic, Pierre Mendès-France. The importance of the Socialist parties is mainly that they may provide a rallying point for a younger generation not bewitched by the Communist legend and myth but nonetheless critical of "capitalist" rule.

THE only French party that can be compared at all with the Communists in discipline and vigor is the Mouvement Républicain Populaire, usually referred to as the M.R.P. and adequately enough described in English as the Christian Democrats. This party, like the Communists, gained greatly in esteem by its role in the Resistance. It became especially popular among women voters by giving critical support in 1946 to the successful campaign to abolish legalized brothels. It has a more effective trade union movement than the Socialists have. It has been pushed back to its original left-wing position by the appearance of probably transient parties that claim to represent General de Gaulle (like the Union for the New Republic). But it was considerably weakened (or purified) by the hiving off of many of its conservative members on the burning question of Algeria.

The Algerian war was to the Christian Democrats (and to Frenchmen and Frenchwomen of all parties) what the Hungarian revolution was to the European Communists: a crisis of conscience. The war, which began in November, 1954, and ended in July, 1962, cost billions of dollars. Nearly half a million French soldiers were kept on continuous duty in Algeria, with disastrous effects on the French contribution to the North Atlantic Treaty Organization. A million and a half Frenchmen served in Algeria during the eight-year war. They were in many cases recalled to service after having already done their ordinary military stint. The conflict was bloody as well as costly. At least 300,000 men were killed—though most were Algerian rebels.

But the war was more than expensive and bloody. It was corrupting. There were many well-authenticated stories of the torturing of prisoners and of savage reprisals. Hope that De Gaulle would bring peace to Algeria was one of the sources of the general's popularity. But peace on what terms? If Algeria determined her own fate, what would happen to the million-odd "colonists" who made up a tenth of the population? Even though many of them were of Spanish, Italian or Maltese origin, they were all "Frenchmen." These questions bitterly divided the people of France.

What the outside world saw as a triumph of General de Gaulle's policy—the peaceful and amicable liquidation of the old empire and the replacement of the loosely federated French Community with a series of independent states —was seen by the fearful inside France as an ominous portent for the future of Algeria. What use was it to impose conditions on Algerian autonomy if it had proved so easy for Tunisia and Morocco to ignore the limitations on their sovereignty and become fully independent? Just as the Algerian war precipitated the crisis that brought the Fifth Republic into existence, Algeria almost spelled its end.

THE Algerian threat could have offset many successes of the new regime. De Gaulle's government has carried out many reforms that are not of the first importance individually but important in the mass. It has dared to tackle some powerful pressure groups. It has immeasurably increased France's international prestige. It has given the French a sense of being led, of being worthily represented, and of having a government with a purpose of its own and the power to plan for the future, not one confined just to the present. But it may be doubted that the French political problem has been solved.

Under De Gaulle, the government of the Fifth Republic has been a personal government, the government of a man completely overshadowing his colleagues. These colleagues have nearly all been specialists of one kind or another, experts of great ability, honesty and public spirit but of little political experience or skill. All fundamental decisions have been made by the president, which means that many have not been made and some that have been made were inconsistent. So far, the government of the Fifth Republic is the government of one man. But it is not the government of a dictator. Fundamental liberties are preserved. The parliament grumbles and resists, and sometimes it forces modifications in presidential policy.

A NEW and unpredictable element was introduced into French politics in 1962 by the constitutional change entrusting election of the president to the popular national vote. Under the law, which De Gaulle had himself sponsored, the general needed more than 50 per cent of the vote to win re-election in 1965. But in the first balloting he received only 44 per cent, a surprise result showing that a clear majority of the French electorate felt dissatisfaction with one or more of his policies.

In the campaigning, five candidates struck hard at De Gaulle's nationalistic stand against a speed-up in European integration. The general's insistence upon an independent French military force was also criticized, even though a French satellite had just been orbited to make France the world's third nation in space. In the runoff election, De Gaulle won, as was expected. But his prestige had been impaired.

General de Gaulle was re-elected at the age of 75 to a seven-year term of office. Should he one day wish to name a successor, he may find that he has lost the power, used so frequently in state affairs since 1958, to make a unilateral choice. The political consciousness of France was vigorously reawakened in 1965. Perhaps this is as well. It was the general himself who said, "No man can be a substitute for the people."

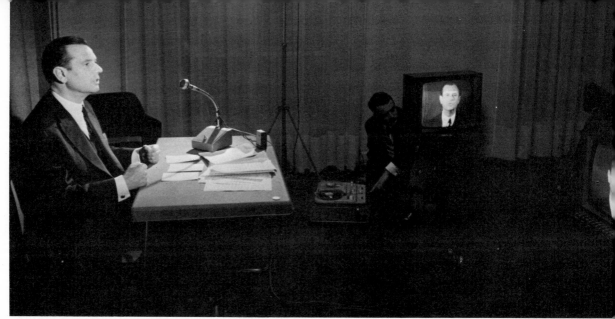

SPEAKING ON TELEVISION, Catholic center candidate Jean Lecanuet, a virtual unknown before the campaign, exploits the youthful good looks that led opponents to dub him "John Fitzgerald Lecanuet." Drawing off 16 per cent of the vote with a pro-NATO, pro-Europe stand, he was instrumental in forcing De Gaulle into a runoff election.

COUNTING VOTES, election officials make their tally at a polling place in Paris. De Gaulle received only 44 per cent of all the ballots but won 55 per cent in the runoff.

CAMPAIGNING AMONG FARMERS, François Mitterand, the runner-up in the election with Socialist and Communist support, promises a better deal for French agriculture.

54

A Government Freely Chosen

In December 1965 French men and women chose their president by direct vote for the first time since 1848. The election was also the first in France to be influenced importantly by television. Six candidates, including General de Gaulle, took equal turns addressing the country on TV. De Gaulle failed to win an absolute majority on the first ballot and was forced to campaign in a runoff election against leftist François Mitterand two weeks later. Critics saw in this a humiliation for the haughty general and a national rejection of his policies. But in an era when parliamentary governments in many parts of the world have been toppled by military men, the French nation had put on a heartening demonstration of democracy alive and working.

Beneath the majestic chandeliers in the great banquet hall of the Elysée Palace, home of French presidents since 1873, General de Gaulle

holds his semiannual press conference in September 1965, discoursing from a thronelike elevation to an audience of a thousand newsmen.

THE POLITICS OF PROTEST *are a continuing reality of French public life. Although France has achieved great prosperity, there are still many who feel that they have not fully shared in the nation's bounty*

A CROWD OF MINEWORKERS employed in the nationalized French coal industry rallies at Les Invalides in Paris during a 1963 strike, hoping to publicize their demand for wages comparable to those received in private industry. Twenty-five per cent of all French workers are in nationalized areas of the economy, hence are state employees.

A SIGN OF RECENT TIMES appears on a street in the industrial city of St. Junien, which has had a Communist administration for more than 40 years. The street was later named again, for a French Communist stalwart. Although the Communist party is declining as a force in national politics, it still regularly polls 20 per cent of the vote.

DRILLING into a mountain slope with jackhammers, workers clear the ground for the huge new Tignes Dam in southeast France, one of the highest dams in Europe.

The Miraculous Recovery

"HAPPY as God in France." This traditional German saying recalls the envy with which, until a century ago, her neighbors looked upon France. She was by far the most populous and powerful state in Europe west of Russia. She stretched from the North Sea to the Mediterranean, from the Rhine to the Atlantic. Only England was comparably fertile, and England was much smaller.

France had everything that her neighbors had: wheat, barley, oats, grapes, apples, oranges, silk, hemp, flax, cattle, abundant forests, widely distributed iron fields and an equable climate. No wonder that in the Middle Ages the French had used the battle cry: "Long live Christ who loves the French!" This treasure house was, by the standard of the times, densely populated, and the population was both industrious and ingenious. Compared with France, such neighboring countries as Germany, Italy and Spain were all terribly handicapped, and the Low Countries and England were greatly inferior in both population and area.

Indeed, one of the principal French troubles in modern times has been the survival of this belief that France was naturally the richest and consequently the most powerful nation in Europe outside of Russia. The country suffered great disasters in the 19th and 20th Centuries, but one of the most widely accepted European beliefs was that she had exceptional powers of recuperation. Disasters that would have destroyed other countries were rapidly recovered from. Thus after her defeat at the hands of Germany in 1871 and the subsequent civil war of the Paris Commune, France not only was able to pay off what was at the time an immense indemnity of one billion dollars but seemed to many spectators basically richer and more stable than victorious Germany.

Even the visible stagnation of her population was seen by many as a good thing. Theorists in Britain and Germany were saying that their own populations were outrunning available resources and that both countries were taking a very great risk in depending on foreign commerce for economic survival. France, if put to it, could keep herself. And despite the political vicissitudes of French governments, French society remained remarkably stable. The French Revolution had greatly accelerated the transfer of land to the peasantry and to the lower middle classes. The French peasant—industrious, thrifty, tenacious and patriotic—was admired by foreign observers like the economist John Stuart Mill. The skill of French craftsmen was esteemed all over the western world.

SOCIAL stability was reflected in dozens of ways. There was little movement of population from one rural area to another. A peasant bought land with his painfully acquired savings; he was very reluctant to sell it and did not in fact regard land simply as an investment of money. For him every acre acquired was a permanent good for himself and his family. One reason for the low French birth rate during the 19th

Century was undoubtedly the desire to avoid breaking up land holdings among several offspring on the death of the owner.

The same prudence was exemplified by the middle class in the family-arranged marriages, which were more often a union of two economic units than the fruit of romantic love. Family discipline was severe. Family unity was imposed both by law and by custom, and the family as a group meant more than father, mother or children individually. In the small towns the local lawyers, notaries, cattle merchants and other businessmen lived an easier life than the peasantry, but they nourished themselves on much the same ideas. For all of them thrift, foresight, unity of the family and the safety and glory of France were primary values.

AND until the outbreak of World War I this system of society, which was based more on social considerations than on economic ones, seemed to serve its purposes well. Although some young people left the land, their departure was slow. Novelists might report on the dreariness of life in a village or a small town, but most of the inhabitants seemed content. And the peasant, either saving his meager gains by putting them in the traditional "woolen sock," lending them to the local notary for local investment, or buying French or foreign government securities hawked by branches of the great chain banks, made France a source of capital for all of Europe.

True, the peasant spent little of his savings on his land and less on his house. And the small craftsman did not think of expanding his business. There was nothing in the atmosphere of a small town to encourage enterprise. Indeed, it could have been argued that France exported too much capital, especially in the form of loans to foreign governments, and invested too little in herself. Nevertheless there was a rapid increase in French industrialization in the period between 1885 and the start of World War I, and even some improvement in French agriculture. This period became known as *la belle époque* —"the good old days"—and although there is a great deal of superficial romanticism about this picture of the France of 50 years ago it does represent a kind of truth.

If the average Frenchman did not live as well as he does today and had far fewer consumer goods, he didn't know what he missed. Tradition made things easier in many ways. The peasant, and often the town worker as well, wore the traditional blue blouse and kept his one good black suit for great occasions. The peasant still wore wooden shoes. In many regions the peasant's wife and daughters had just one party dress in the local style; you could tell what part of Brittany a woman came from, for example, by her costume.

THE middle classes of the towns were not as frugal as the peasants but they were undeniably thrifty. They had (and still have) a much narrower social life than the English, not to speak of the Americans. They spent less time and money in general sociability. Sport, apart from hunting, was unfamiliar to them. Theirs was a way of life that made endless, grinding industry understandable and natural. Not much progress was expected, and the salvation of the family patrimony was the typical aim of the head of the family. To accomplish this much —to save his assets for his children, possibly to help them move on a little in the world toward a profession or a job in the government— was the first duty of a father.

One of France's psychological problems today is a lingering memory, especially in the older generations and especially in the countryside, of a way of life that was, in fact, much harder than it seems in retrospect, but which seems normal and right to those who remember it. In that world the small farmer, the small shopkeeper or craftsman, the minor professional man was the ideal citizen. Expansion as such might be actually dangerous, since it could push aside some worthy if unenterprising friends or kinsmen. Today in rural France and in the small towns it is still possible to find this attitude, but justification for it was destroyed by the catastrophes of this century, even though the awareness of

that destruction took a long time to sink in.

First of all, the war of 1914–1918 not only inflicted immense losses on France, but inflicted those losses on two of the most valuable sectors of the French economy. It was across the most modern and some of the most fertile parts of France that the armies fought. It was on the young peasants that the greatest burden of death fell. France by 1919 had lost much of her modern capital equipment and machinery, many of her mines and transportation facilities and, what was far worse, more than 1,400,000 dead—and proportionately the greater part of the dead were peasants. French rural life has never really recovered from the bloodletting of World War I and the subsequent emigration to the cities. The impoverishment of a great deal of rural France today, the emptiness of many regions, was caused by this disaster.

Secondly, the cost of reconstructing the devastated areas used up most of France's capital resources, leaving little for expansion. Furthermore, French credit was badly shaken by the war. When the franc was finally stabilized in 1926 it was at a fifth of its prewar value. The old simple belief in thrift and prudence and in French solvency was badly shaken. Some economic expansion did take place up to 1929, but after the beginning of the Great Depression the French economy grew more and more stagnant.

BY 1939 France was hardly any richer than she had been in 1914. In some ways, especially in the potential represented by the birth rate, she was a great deal poorer. She had admittedly escaped some of the Depression's worst features like the mass unemployment of Britain, the United States and Germany. But her economic life was at a low ebb as she entered World War II.

By then the old wealth of France was not as important as it had been. France could not produce wheat as cheaply as Canada. Her industrial equipment was becoming increasingly out of date. She had suffered all through the 19th and early 20th Centuries from a coal supply that was both poor in quality (there was hardly any

PRODUCTS OF FRANCE are portrayed on the map above, which reveals the preponderance of both heavy industry and agricultural wealth in the North. Ships indicate busy seaports. Top wine regions are Bordeaux, Champagne, Burgundy; others are the Loire Valley, Alsace, Provence. Most hydroelectric power originates in the southeast.

good coking coal at all) and widely scattered in small mining areas. This in turn helped bring about a dissipation of industry in small units, poorly located from a competitive standpoint. Most of these small and declining industrial areas were in the South, which was also agriculturally the most backward part of France.

THERE were, of course, some bright spots in the economic picture. There was a good, if not first-class, coal field in the North, the basis for an important industrial area. Two British metallurgists had discovered a method of purifying the otherwise unusable iron ore of Lorraine, and France had become one of the biggest iron ore producers in the world, though more an exporter of ore to Germany and the Low Countries than a manufacturer of steel at home. But with competition virtually excluded both by high tariffs and by quotas, and with the franc being kept at an artificially high valuation which hampered exports, France seemed to have withdrawn from the modern industrial world. Even in the fields in which she had been a pioneer—in the automobile industry, for instance—her slow expansion disappointed some of the hopes raised in the early part of the century. The old virtues, habits, fears and hopes seemed irrelevant in the world of Hitler's Germany and Franklin Roosevelt's New Deal. The younger generation began to look abroad to the United States, to Russia, to Britain, even to Germany. And then came the catastrophe of 1940–1945.

The France of 1945 was far poorer even than the France of 1939. Fighting had taken place in almost every region. More than 440,000 houses were completely destroyed and another 1,344,000 damaged. Some 135,000 farm buildings were damaged or demolished. More than 55,000 commercial and industrial buildings were lost. Four fifths of the railway engines and almost two thirds of the freight cars were destroyed or severely damaged. And the French gold reserve, which had been so treasured and which had weighed nearly 5,000 tons in 1932, was down to 487 tons in 1948. Not until 1951 did the real wages of the French worker reach the not very high levels of 1938. Moreover, the financing of French recovery was made possible only by lavish injections of American aid in gifts, loans and military expenditures (since 1945 the United States has pumped nearly 10 billion dollars into France). The clacking sound in the Paris streets of the wooden-soled shoes worn by Frenchwomen in the grim years of 1944 and 1945 was perhaps as good a symbol as any of the destitution of the country.

During the war, both inside France and outside it in exile, Frenchmen had been pondering the problem of the future of France and trying to assess the causes of the great disaster. It was the conviction of many Frenchmen that the country's entire economic structure had to be recast, that many of the habits which had made France stable and so agreeable to live in were intolerable in a modern world. Of those who believed this, by far the most important was a remarkably farsighted thinker named Jean Monnet, who had spent part of the war in the United States. France, said Monnet, would have to be dragged into the 20th Century, or she would slip into a permanent decline.

THIS view was debated in Washington, in London, in Algiers. It was also debated underground in France. The wartime government of Marshal Pétain had deliberately encouraged the "old France" of peasants and small craftsmen. It had preached "back to the land" and had seemed prepared to let France be the back garden of a Europe dominated by a highly industrialized Germany. And there were patriotic Frenchmen who thought that the best thing France could do was apply her meager capital resources to the improvement of her agriculture.

Such, however, was not the view of the new government which took over France after 1944, nor of Monnet, who became the head of the General Planning Commission. It was the opinion of Monnet and his colleagues that only by rapid industrialization could France deal with the problem of her poverty. The idea of economic planning was much in the air. It was a vague idea and meant one thing to a confirmed

Communist and another to a businessman. But it involved as a minimum the direction of the main trends of investment by the state, and the main investment trends in Monnet's proposal were directed toward heavy industry: steel, machinery, automobiles, transportation and power. French agriculture needed capital too, but it would not get top priority.

INEVITABLY the capital had first of all to come from the state—and therefore, to a large extent, from the United States. The Paris money market, disorganized by war, occupation and inflation, was in no condition to make the necessary funds available. Immediately after the war there had been a wave of nationalizations, a wave made necessary more by political hostility to big business than by absolute economic need.

The railways had been placed under government control before the war, and some degree of government control had been exercised over the Bank of France. The aircraft-manufacturing and munitions industries had been nationalized in the late 1930s. Now the Bank of France, the four biggest commercial banks, the biggest insurance companies, the coal, gas and electricity industries and the Renault automobile company were all nationalized. But very important sectors of French industry remained free of direct government supervision, and in many instances profits were plowed back so as to provide the badly needed capital for expansion.

In this flurry of investment and economic development, great mistakes were undoubtedly made. Repeated devaluations of the franc have made it difficult to estimate the true cost of the transformation of French heavy industry. But by 1953 the Monnet Plan, the first great shot in the arm, had been put into effect and the France that had been so desperately impoverished in 1945 was already a very different and vastly improved country.

The second plan, initiated in 1954 and called the Hirsch Plan after its chief, was not so exclusively directed to increasing heavy industrial equipment. Lighter industries and agriculture now received a large share of the government's

bounty, and with the general recovery private business became more important.

But for good or ill the biggest single force working on the French economy since the end of the last war has been the French state, and the state could not have supported this role but for the generosity of the American government. French politicians of the Left, most but not all of them Communists, tried and had some success in concealing this truth from a great many French people, but for a great many more the lesson has been learned: the way into the modern world was by "Americanization."

"Americanization" is a term that is used both to praise and to condemn, and condemnation comes both from old-fashioned French people and from the Left. The old-fashioned people, especially in the small towns and rural areas, blame everything they dislike, especially in the younger generation, on Americanization. They see it, rightly enough, as a revolutionary force upsetting the traditional concepts of family and marriage, and as an enemy of the "sweetness of life" which they attribute to the old France. The Communists see it as the chief means of capitalist seduction. To them it is an evil force which diverts the young from the vision of a class war leading to an eventual heaven of justice, and attracts them to a more attainable heaven of high production and high consumption.

AMERICANIZATION shows up not only in the shifting pattern of French consumption and in the increasing abandonment of the "make do and mend" philosophy of French peasant tradition in favor of ever-increasing satisfaction of sometimes artificial needs, but also in the appearance of a new type of French businessman. The new man often belongs to the class who call themselves the *jeunes patrons*, or young bosses. Many of the young bosses have been to American business schools and, even if they have not, are dazzled by American methods. They realize that in a country with a rising population the place of the old unexpanding family firm is threatened. France must expand and expand rapidly, they maintain, to provide employment for the rising population and markets for what the new population produces.

They are conscious, too, that they have much to learn in the field of labor relations and in the province of projecting a "public image" of the firm. They know that they must improve the relationship between themselves and their workers. They envy the degree to which the American worker is persuaded that he shares in the benefits of American production. They think, and think rightly, that the spread of such an attitude in France would produce great economic as well as social gains.

THE ambitions of the young bosses would be meaningless if France were not, in fact, producing a much bigger cake to divide. From the boom year of 1929 French industrial production had dropped 20 per cent by 1938 and 76 per cent by the end of the war. But today it is more than double the 1929 level. The boom has been uneven, and in 1963 the government deliberately checked it because of inflationary pressures. Nonetheless, steel production has doubled the previous high of 1929. Automobile and truck production is six times as great, running to more than 1,600,000 units in 1964. The use of electricity has more than quadrupled.

The French railways are now the world's greatest pioneers in electrification, and French methods of cutting electrification costs are admired in other busy railroading countries. France is much more competitive in the international market than she once was. Again, to reiterate the theme, you can see in France some of the most modern technical installations in the world—like the great power dams at Tignes and Donzère-Mondragon in the southeast—and some of the most obsolete plants still in operation in the western world.

Even nature has taken a hand in underlining this contrast. The great natural gas field at Lacq in the foothills of the Pyrenees has favored the growth of the petrochemical industry in the neighborhood and elsewhere—for the Lacq pipeline has already reached Paris and Lyons. It has also accelerated the decline of the small and uneconomic French coal fields, which are losing out to hydroelectric power and oil as well as to natural gas.

There is now a car for every seven French people (in 1950 the ratio was 1 to 28), and although only a minority of workers own automobiles the minority is growing. A car—probably second-hand—is now the symbol of the worker's liberation from his old status. At any rate, the young French worker today has before him the possibility of a more abundant life, and if there is a falling-off in revolutionary enthusiasm—and there is—this is one reason for it.

It must be remembered, however, that not only has the economic transformation of France been mainly industrial and not agricultural, but the social structure of France still shows some disturbing weaknesses. French public finance had been extravagant and badly managed for nearly two generations. The adoption of the "new franc" in 1960—the franc is now worth about 20 cents—represented the government's bold gamble that the repeated devaluations which had robbed so many millions of Frenchmen since 1914 were finally coming to an end. So far, the gamble has come off and French finances are healthier than at any time since 1914.

THE French people have also been promised tax reforms, which are equally desirable but much harder to carry out. It is often said that the Frenchman does not pay taxes. He does. He is as highly taxed as the Englishman and more highly taxed than the American. But the incidence of taxation falls very arbitrarily on him. An income tax was introduced in 1917, but it has never become the main support of government finance as in the United States and Great Britain. The system favors the small shopkeeper, the peasant and the craftsman. It does not favor the salaried and wage earning classes. Its complications, and a tradition of tax evasion, make the administering of tax laws extremely difficult, and the government does not have enough tax officials to make sure that the laws really are being enforced.

Even more demoralizing than the impact of

the tax system is the serious shortage of housing. To this deplorable fact many evils can be imputed. Social discontent and envy are certainly greatly increased by the abominable conditions in which many French people have to live, especially the many young people who are trying to start homes of their own. The alcoholism which is a curse of some areas of France is in part explained by bad housing conditions, for the café is a natural refuge from the slum. France is one of the worst-housed countries in western Europe, and this situation figured importantly in the 1965 election.

Although France has known a nearly continuous economic boom since 1954, her housing program has been grossly inadequate. Most rural houses are extremely old, and even in Paris the average age of a dwelling is almost 80 years. Nearly a quarter of the houses in France have no inside water supply. Only one in four dwellings has a bath or shower.

THERE are several reasons for this great national scandal. The destruction resulting from the two great wars reduced an already inadequate housing stock. Then a policy of rent control, adopted in World War I and continued with minor modifications down to the present day, turned renting into economic folly. Property owners often receive less in rent than the actual cost of keeping a building in a minimum state of repair.

In addition, there is the Frenchman's own attitude toward housing. Traditionally he has spent more of his income on food and drink—and, latterly, on a car—than on rent or for the purchase of better housing. That attitude is now changing, but even those who want a better house may not be able to buy it because mortgage money is hard to obtain. Moreover, the French building industry is fantastically old-fashioned. There are around 200,000 building "firms" consisting most often of an employer and one or two workmen. These tiny organizations have among them neither the capital nor the equipment to meet the country's housing needs. It is calculated that at the present rate of

building, France will take at least 10 years to meet her immediate housing needs.

If building and housing are one of the dark sectors of the French economy, another is the system of retail distribution. True, the modern world is attacking the old French distribution system. Even before the war, there were great grocery chain stores; and in recent years *prix-fixe* (five-and-ten) stores have spread, as supermarkets now are. But even today there is nearly one shop for every 60 Frenchmen. Not only does this waste labor—more than a million people serve in shops—but keeping so many tiny establishments in existence requires that profit margins be excessively large.

The entire French economy, in fact, is full of built-in obstacles to efficiency. It has long been a tradition that the state should protect the small man and, if necessary, compensate him for the results of his competitive weakness. Humanly enough, the shopkeeper is reluctant to face the fact that he often has no real economic justification for being in business at all, and he regards as an outrage the chain store, price cutting and indeed most of what an American would think of as the legitimate results of competition. Meanwhile the French worker, the salaried employee, and the modern and efficient business organization must carry the burden of these obsolescent economic units.

IT was the contrast between a booming commercial system on the one hand and a decaying feudalism and an increasingly bankrupt government on the other that in large part brought about the great revolutionary crisis of 1789. Many of the institutions, economic and legal, created by the Revolution are now as obsolete as feudalism was then. The middle classes or "Third Estate" in 1789 finally lost patience with the old order that was an obstacle to expansion. Today a new France is challenging the old order and demanding not only equality but supremacy. There can be very little doubt that she will win. The great question is by what means and at what cost—a cost to be measured not only in money but in social peace.

Puffing away contentedly beside his "No Credit" sign, the tobacconist of a village in Normandy waits for business to come his way.

Clues to a Booming Economy

The traditional French shopkeeper or small businessman of the past was cautious, hardheaded and suspicious of new merchandising methods. There are still many such die-hards around, like the petty tobacconist above, but for the most part they have been engulfed in the wave of modernization now sweeping France. In a dramatic comeback from the disaster of World War II the country has remodeled its economy and, spurred by a new breed of forward-looking, imaginative businessmen, has achieved some notable industrial and technological triumphs.

UNORTHODOX DAM, the bosomy Barrage de la Girotte in the French Alps consists of multiple arches of reinforced concrete, which is both economical and strong.

PIONEERING PLANE, the Caravelle (*below*) was the first medium-range jet in airline service. Here soldiers line up to greet De Gaulle, arriving in Algiers via the jet.

TECHNICAL GAINS *have paced France's postwar economic progress. A willingness to experiment with new building methods, radical engineering concepts and complex scientific processes has produced marvels of modern technology*

DESERT OIL, a bonanza of the Sahara wastelands, is pumped from lonely wells (*rear*). Prospected for 11 years, oil gushes to the Mediterranean through a 175-mile pipeline under the sands.

SHIPPING *provides the lifeblood of French economic health—from the humble barges that move goods through a vast network of inland waterways to the giant ocean liners of the transatlantic trade*

VITAL RIVER, the Seine flows placidly through Paris carrying a tremendous amount of water traffic. France's most important navigable river, it has made Paris a major port.

LOADED BARGE moves along a quiet, poplar-lined canal in southern France. More than 6,000 canals and navigable rivers give commercial access to every region of France.

THE S.S. "FRANCE," pride of the French merchant fleet, churns at a steady 30 knots toward Le Havre, bearing 2,000 passengers in solid comfort from New York. The 1,035-foot ship, which began service in 1962, incorporates many scientific advances in design, while maintaining an old French Line tradition of superb cuisine afloat.

FASHION AND TOURISM *are two of France's most lucrative businesses. In July, buyers converge on Paris for the fall showings of the famous dress houses, while sun bathers converge on the beaches of the Riviera*

BEFORE A SHOWING, a model for the successful House of Balmain dresses amid backstage clutter. The styles set by some 20 top Paris couturiers are copied everywhere.

ON THE SHOREFRONT of Juan-les-Pins, modern beach hotels overlook a strip of Mediterranean sand which is thronged with vacationers from all parts of the world.

INDUSTRY'S BOOM *got under way in the late 1940s. Sparked by government planning and by enterprising business management, the recovery has brought revolutionary changes to the French economy*

BIGGEST BUSINESS, the Renault automobile company is France's largest single industrial enterprise. At a plant near Paris (*above*) the production line carries bodies for the company's successful Dauphine model. Renault also produces trucks, machine tools, paints, plastics and ball bearings.

MORE STEEL for France has come in recent years from the great Lorraine iron ore fields, where a worker (*left*) taps an open hearth furnace. The Lorraine fields, which supply 94 per cent of France's ore, are the most important in Europe.

INLAND PORT and freight center, Strasbourg (*below*) lies at the junction of the Rhine-Marne Canal (*top left*) and the River Ill. The city handles much of the iron ore and steel of Lorraine. In the foreground are gasoline storage tanks.

POWER SOURCE, a great new processing plant for natural gas glistens in the night near Lacq. Here in the Pyrenees gas was discovered in 1951, bringing about a major postwar economic development. Gas is piped from here to Paris, Nantes and Lyons, and a new petrochemical industry has risen nearby.

VINEYARD'S YIELD, a bunch
of fresh white grapes which
will go into making brandy
is admired by a comely vin-
tager who wears the head-
dress of the Cognac region.

5

New Horizons Beckoning the Farmer

FROM Roman times down to this century, the representative Frenchman was the peasant. He was "Jacques Bonhomme" ("James Goodfellow"). On his labors the whole prosperity of France depended, and he was the object of a great deal of rather patronizing praise from his social and economic superiors. Yet the fact that during the Middle Ages the word *jacquerie* signified a savage peasant revolt against feudal oppression shows that the peasant was not always rewarded as he thought he should have been.

Today, in addition to his genuine economic and social problems, the French peasant or farmer has to face the fact that he is no longer economically or socially as important as he used to be. For although a fifth of France's working population is on the land, farmers receive only a twelfth of the national income. But more important, farming, and above all small-scale farming, is visibly in decline as a way of life, and

81

the French countryside is going through a revolution as important as, and far more painful than, the revolution that is transforming the industrial areas.

In many ways the peasant was the chief gainer from the 1789 Revolution. He certainly thought that he was, and he had good reason for thinking so. He had been freed from a great number of burdensome and humiliating obligations to the nobility. He became, in his own eyes, a full citizen for the first time. And although the picture of the lands held by the nobility and the church all passing into the hands of the peasants is false, the Revolution did bring a considerable increase in peasant land ownership. The small family farm was considered by most Frenchmen to be the natural basis of the economy and the source of social and economic stability.

BOTH of these roles are called into question today. In the first place, the population employed on the land has gone down in this century by a third. About a million and a half people have left the farms since the end of World War II, and yet it is estimated by some agricultural economists that there are a million too many still on the land.

Most of the farms are too small to provide a decent livelihood even if the peasant farmer has capital, is willing to spend it and has adequate technical knowledge. And in a great part of France none of these conditions is met. Thirty-five per cent of French farms are under 12 acres, and these are obviously impractical units. Of the total number of farms almost 80 per cent are less than 50 acres. Only on a farm of about 50 acres or more is it practical to use modern equipment, like a full-time tractor. But even 50 acres is not an adequate unit for very advanced, highly capitalized farming.

The situation in many regions of France is a good deal worse than even the figures suggest. For very often a small farm consists not of a continuous area of land, but of a number of strips scattered all over the commune. This fragmentation of the land is one of the less desirable results of the Revolution, for the inheritance laws passed at that time required parents to bequeath specified portions of their property to each child instead of leaving it all to the eldest. Before the Revolution, peasants under the general direction of a landlord cultivated the same crops according to uniform rotation schedules. After the Revolution each peasant owner was free to farm as he liked, and the discipline of the old order disappeared. Obviously a farmer whose 12 or 14 acres are in five or six different strips cannot practice a very advanced form of agriculture. He spends much of his time simply walking from one strip to another and cannot expect to make anything but a bare living.

Yet the changes that are transforming France can be seen at work even in backward regions. For one thing, it is harder and harder to hire labor, and so the farmers want more and more to obtain the new machinery which can profitably be used only on farms composed of contiguous fields. Since World War II the French government has done much to encourage the "reassembling" of farms into workable units. This is a job requiring not only a high degree of technical skill but also considerable tact, for it is often hard to persuade a farmer that he has been offered a fair exchange. It sometimes takes as much as two or three years for the complicated change to be effected.

TRUE, even the strip system did not always work so badly, for some farmers rented strips from their neighbors and worked them as adjoining fields. But the French farmer does not usually see his land holdings in terms of a rational money economy. A visitor to central France was recently astonished to learn that a woman of his acquaintance, one of the richest women in France, could not buy her son more than a single farm of about 135 acres because none of the owners of adjoining farms would sell. Even in the presumably sophisticated regions near Paris this obstinate clinging to the land prevents its full economic use.

The new technology, however, continues to flood in. First of all, farmers are showing greater readiness to spend money on improving the capital equipment of their farms than they used to. Perhaps inflation has persuaded them that modern machinery is a better investment than stacks of paper money. At any rate, there are now almost a million tractors in use on French farms, as compared with 144,000 in 1950. Some economists think this indicates an excessive number of tractors for a country that has so many farms of much less than 100 acres.

There is also an increased use of artificial fertilizers and a consequent rapid increase in crop yield. Some areas once considered almost worthless have been brought into cultivation through the application of soil chemistry based on American experiments, and some backward areas have been revitalized through the enterprise of repatriated colonials from Algeria and Indochina. The government has subsidized model farms and model villages whose demonstrations of new methods have shaken the conservatism and skepticism of the French farmer. Yet there are far too few trained farm experts in France to give the peasant the lead he needs.

In some regions the Catholic Church has done as much as the state to improve farming methods and to make it possible and attractive for young people to stay on the land. French farmers and agricultural experts have profited greatly by U.S. government-sponsored visits to America, but one exceptionally competent farmer reported that he had learned much more from the methods of the American South than from what he was shown in Minnesota and Iowa. For the southern U.S. farmer, like the representative French farmer, has to make do with far less capital equipment than is in common use in the northern American farm states.

THERE is, of course, a great deal of extremely advanced farming in France which pays off handsomely. The best examples are the great vineyards. In her wine resources, as in many of her other natural assets, France is highly favored by nature. She can produce almost all the kinds of wine that her neighbors—Germany, Italy and Spain—can produce and many that they cannot. Most of the world's famous wines are French.

A vineyard like the Romanée-Conti in Burgundy, which comprises only four and a half acres, is nearly as valuable as if its land were located in downtown Chicago. The elegance of the wines of another Burgundian vineyard, the Clos Vougeot, inspired one of Napoleon's colonels to order a drum roll when his column passed its gates. French military units still present arms when passing by there.

The most famous vineyards, of course, are not confined to Burgundy. For many hundreds of years the country around Bordeaux has been an exporter of expensive wine to England as well as to many other countries. The discovery in the 17th Century of a way of making the wine of Champagne sparkle created a great luxury wine which bears the name of its native province. Other celebrated winegrowing areas are the Rhône and Loire valleys.

BUT it is in the French wine industry that some of the problems of French agriculture —especially agriculture in the South—can best be seen. For just as the American South has its dominant cotton crop, the French South has its dominant crop, wine. Most of the southern wine is not the high-priced luxury product of Burgundy or Bordeaux. It is what the French call *vin ordinaire*, the daily drink of men, women—and children. It is very often produced on small tracts by poor farmers, who are at the mercy of a crop that is peculiarly susceptible to the seasons. In a bad year, the rich and prudent wine producers of Burgundy will refuse to damage the reputation of their well-known wines by putting them on the market under their traditional labels. But while the peasant wine maker of the South has no brand name to protect, he has to endure the competition of the mass-producing vineyards of Algeria. The government tries to maintain prices, but in this century the small wine producer has often felt that things were moving against him.

The other great basic crop of France, as sacred as wine in French mythology, is wheat. Here France has very great advantages over her European neighbors, for large areas of the country are admirably adapted to wheat growing. And although the acreage planted in wheat has fallen off sharply in this century, the yield per acre has risen rapidly because of improved farming methods. France indeed could, if her neighbors let her, undersell her European competitors, and she is one of the few countries of western Europe that can produce enough wheat for her own needs. Her production of sugar beets is also very efficient. Other crops like barley, corn and rice have increased in importance in recent years, but the great shift in French agricultural practice has been from raising crops to raising cattle.

In livestock production France again is greatly favored, both by soil types and by climate. The French eat much more meat than they used to and many old-fashioned Frenchmen have complained that the housewife today will not buy the cheaper cuts and display her traditional culinary dexterity in making them palatable.

IT is not only in her disdain for cheap cuts of meat that the French housewife—even the farmer's wife—shows the influence of the modern world. If her husband sometimes spends more than is wise on agricultural machinery, the wife is not content with the primitive domestic equipment that was good enough for her mother. A visitor to a part of France where some of the most profitable beef cattle are raised was astonished to see so many washing machines on sale at the local fair. He knew that most of the villages in the area had no running water. His host explained the mystery. "Women have now got the vote," he said, "and if half a dozen women in a village buy washing machines, they will see that the village council does something about a piped water supply."

In many parts of rural France life has been transformed for the better in a way almost as revolutionary as the transformation of industry. But there remain some areas about whose future it is not possible to be optimistic. Some of these are intrinsically poor—mountainous, barren, often with a severe climate that makes the raising of profitable crops impossible. Others are calamitously underpopulated, with hardly

any farmers under 50 years of age. What few children there are leave for the big cities.

It seems easy on paper to suggest the transfer of the population of some overpopulated rural regions to the areas that have been bled white. The government has, in fact, sponsored such a program. But the French farmer is extremely reluctant to leave his own countryside. He may quit the land entirely and move to Paris or another city, but he will be very reluctant to move 20 or 30 miles to better farming opportunities.

THERE is no doubt that if the rural population of France were redistributed it might be stabilized at about its present level. Under such circumstances the very rapid increase in the technical efficiency of French farming and the real, if not very rapid, progress in creating united farms might cause French agricultural production, which has already increased dramatically, to continue to rise. France could be a more important supplier for her European neighbors if she could exploit her agricultural resources to the fullest. Among the countries of western Europe she has the largest potential for increased food production.

But the French peasant will never again be the representative Frenchman, nor will France again be mainly a producer of wheat, wine and meat. The great decision made after the end of the last war to plunge into industrialization cannot be reversed. What can be done is to try to raise the level of French agriculture to that of its most efficient units, and some of these are very efficient indeed.

The extension of hydroelectric power and the discovery of natural gas at Lacq have made certain backward regions much more attractive to industry, and the government has been making some efforts to divert industry away from the Paris region to handicapped areas like Brittany. Another neglected region, the Camargue west of Marseilles, has recently become an important rice producer. There is plenty of health in the French agricultural system, despite the backwardness and decline of many districts. To be sure, just as there are too many shopkeepers in France, so there are too many middlemen between the farmer and the market, and the farmer's slowness in organizing marketing cooperatives makes him a victim of these middlemen. But the French farmer today has another source of hope, for he shares with the French businessman a renewed expectation that comes from the major economic development of post-war Europe: the Common Market.

IN the general ruin of western and central Europe that was visible in 1945, some Europeans, snatching hope from apparent grounds for despair, began preaching the doctrine of a united Europe. Although this doctrine received much enthusiastic support, in its political form it has not yet had much practical success. But the idea was abroad that a Europe divided into small, mutually hostile states could have no serious future.

As European economic recovery proceeded and as it became certain that Europe would live, the idea of an economic union grew in attraction. Pan-European economic institutions with varying degrees of power and utility were presently created, the most important being the European Coal and Steel Community or "Coal and Steel Pool" entered into by France, West Germany, Belgium, Luxembourg, the Netherlands and Italy in 1951. Western Europe, the greatest industrial powerhouse in the world after the United States and the Russian bloc, had had its recovery delayed not merely by tariffs but by quotas, currency controls and differential freight rates. The object of the Pool was to remove these obstacles in the case of coal and steel and allow modern technology to act freely. The Pool succeeded in breaking down trade barriers, although it has been hampered by the surplus of unsalable coal which afflicts most of Europe, above all Belgium.

An even greater and wider idea of economic cooperation was being urged in the 1950s by that indefatigable salesman of ideas, the French economist Jean Monnet, the man who had originally conceived of the Coal and Steel Pool. More publicly, and very effectively, the idea of a European economic union that might lead to later political unification was preached by Robert Schuman, France's foreign minister from 1948 to 1953. There were kindred spirits in other European countries, notably Chancellor Konrad Adenauer in West Germany and Premier Alcide de Gasperi in Italy.

It was hopes of the kind shared by these three men that led to the Treaty of Rome (1957) in which France, West Germany, Italy, Belgium, Luxembourg and the Netherlands agreed to establish a European Economic Community or "Common Market." Inside this Common Market there would ultimately be neither tariffs nor quotas, and around it would be a uniform tariff barrier. For, as a Frenchman put it, "This is a club. Only members get the privileges." For a long time Britain refused to consider joining. When she did apply, she was vetoed by De Gaulle who made it plain that his objections were not economic but political, that Britain was not sufficiently European-minded and was too much a satellite of the United States.

WITHIN the fence of the Common Market today is an industrial potential and a population nearly equal to that of the United States. Naturally, it was impossible to sweep away all the internal barriers at once. Each country had its own vested interests to protect. But progress toward the elimination of the barriers is going on much more rapidly than the most optimistic dared to hope. The Common Market, which went into effect in 1959 with the first in a projected series of tariff and quota relaxations, has already seriously altered world trade patterns. Trade among Common Market nations is growing much more rapidly than trade with the outside world. So is industrial production. A great new economic giant has, in fact, been born and is rapidly growing up.

There have been the usual difficulties of childhood and adolescence. The Coal and Steel Pool had run into them when it eliminated uneconomic units like some French coal mines and small steel plants. Many French industries feared German industrial competition, and German agriculture feared French competition. But the die is cast. In both France and West Germany, old habits and old wasteful forms of production are dying before the impact of a new era.

There are other beneficial effects. American companies, faced with the tariff barrier, are acting on the old maxim, "If you can't beat 'em, join 'em." They are investing in plants inside the Common Market area, many of them in France.

THE same wind of change has been blowing through what was the French Empire, renamed the French Union at the end of World War II and later called the French Community. The old empire was a closed economic system in which most French-manufactured goods were protected against foreign competition, and raw materials from the empire had a privileged position in France. But except in North Africa and in Indochina there was little investment from France, and after World War II the backwardness of the colonies of "Black Africa" became a scandal. Since then the French government has invested well over two billion dollars in French-speaking Black Africa, and the economic health of these areas, most of which are now independent, has been vastly improved.

Now that these regions are self-governing, however, they cannot be tied to the French economy by the old political methods. The French, indeed, are anxious to get other European countries to invest in the newly independent republics and to encourage ties between the former French colonies and the Common Market. This cannot be done without some serious shocks to both sides. For if the French used to get preferential treatment in the old colonies, some of these colonies also got preferential treatment in France herself. But the prospect of access to the Common Market allays many fears of economic isolation.

Among other new natural resources available to France is oil. Continental France now produces 2,850,000 tons of oil a year and hopes to increase the yield through a full-scale exploitation of four oil fields near the once stagnant city of Bordeaux. But the dream that has dazzled the French has been oil in the Sahara.

The dreamers established at least one thing: there is a great deal of oil in the Sahara. Under an agreement with the government of independent Algeria, France has been developing and exploiting this oil. With great courage and technical ingenuity, and in the face of immense natural difficulties, the French have brought in two big oil fields. Already the Sahara has become a major producer. Two pipelines to the Mediterranean Sea have been completed for carrying the crude oil to tankers. Sahara oil is potentially an important factor in the world oil market and an ace in the hole for France. True, it is not suitable for all the needs of France's industry, but the French hope to exchange some of it for heavier oil. They also hope to use it to strengthen their position in the Common Market. A pipeline brings oil from Marseilles to Karlsruhe in Germany and the Rhine port of Strasbourg has become an important oil refining center.

FOR years, the prospects of Sahara oil were threatened by the Algerian war. The pipeline had to be guarded against Algerian rebels. Now that Algeria has established her independence, France must continue to bargain with the Algerian government. The oil itself may do something to relieve the desperate poverty of Algeria, and here again the economic gains depend on political stability.

Even if the Sahara oil should prove to be what one critical Frenchman has called "the Rhinegold," costing more than it brings in, all the forces in the field of industry, all the new technical and competitive forces in agriculture are driving France faster and faster along new roads. They are driving her toward a policy of high production and of less care for the competitively feeble, and toward closer and closer economic and probably political integration with her neighbors—above all with her former rival and enemy, West Germany. Culinary metaphors are always in order in discussing French affairs. The omelette of integration is not yet made, but the eggs are broken for good.

Scything and binding wheat by hand, a farmer and his wife employ the age-old agricultural methods which are fated to disappear.

Gathering a Matchless Bounty

Harvest time, when the golden wheat is brought in and the grapes plucked from the celebrated vines, means two things in France today. First of all it denotes the slow but inexorable transformation taking place on French farmlands, with new ways replacing old and the small, widely separated and impractical strips being consolidated into more efficient and more profitable larger units. Secondly it indicates, as always, the incomparable bounty which ends up being served proudly on the tables of France: a feast of food and wine unsurpassed anywhere on earth.

SNUFFLING A TRUFFLE, Alain Pebeyre exhibits distinct pleasure as he savors one of the products processed by the company he heads in Cahors. Truffles, black fungi that grow under the ground, are called "diamonds of the kitchen" because of the superb flavor they add to dishes like *pâté de foie gras*, poultry stuffing and omelets.

FOOD SPECIALTIES *have made many a small French town or port familiar to the world's gourmets, and have helped give French cooking its great reputation for subtlety and variety of flavor*

CHEESE is aged in clean, vaulted caves in Roquefort in southern France. By French law only the cheese actually produced within the town of Roquefort itself can be sold under that designation.

SARDINES are gathered during the night off the Brittany coast. Sardine fishing is confined to the warmer waters south of the Breton peninsula. The large lights on the boats serve to attract the fish.

A patchwork of vineyards rises above the town of Ribeauville in Alsace, an important wine-producing region since the days of the

LUXURIANT VINE offers up its grapes near Avignon in Provence. Châteauneuf-du-Pape wines of this region were introduced by Pope Clement V while he was in Avignon.

WINES *are France's best-known export. The government enforces rigid cultivation requirements to ensure the high quality of the varieties it allows to be shipped abroad*

Romans, who brought the first vine stalks from Italy.

MASSIVE CASKS of an *apéritif* called Byrrh age in the cellars of the Violet Frères company in the Pyrenees. Byrrh is a form of vermouth that has been mixed with herbs and other natural flavorings.

SKILLED BOTTLER, called a *décanteur*, transfers wine from casks in the cellars of the J. Calvet company in Beaune, a town in Burgundy. Calvet is a big shipper of Burgundy and Bordeaux wines.

91

FOOD MARKETS, *though popular among housewives and tourists, are inefficiently organized and badly in need of modernization. There are too many middlemen between the farmer and the eventual consumer, and there are far too many small and unprofitable stores*

HORSEMEAT SHOP in Paris, which proclaims its identity with a golden horse's head, exists to sell only its one product. Hundreds of Paris butcher shops sell horsemeat.

DISTRIBUTION CENTER for all France is Les Halles (the markets), an antiquated merchandising complex in Paris. The state will replace it with regional shopping centers.

FABULOUS RESTAURANTS, *a special French tradition, boast master chefs who consider cooking a fine art. Sauces, spices and herbs are used liberally and complex dishes are served with an eye to drama*

THE PYRAMIDE, in Vienne just south of Lyons, has been called the "loftiest tabernacle of gastronomy in France." Its noted dishes include *langouste*, or crayfish (*center*).

THE TOUR D'ARGENT (*opposite*), one of the most celebrated eating places in Paris, is especially known for its pressed duck. Diners get a superb view of Notre Dame.

A LAVISH DINNER is available to guests at the Hôtel des Montgomery in Pontorson, Normandy (*opposite*), where a waiter prepares the *homard* served *flambé* in Armagnac.

A FAMILY MEAL nears completion in the kitchen of a private home, as an elderly woman tests the duck with the thoughtful care that has always marked French cooking.

As their ancestors have done for centuries, students from the Sorbonne gather in a smoke-filled Left Bank café after classes to discuss and

debate the vital philosophical and political questions of the day.

6

A Flourishing Marketplace of Ideas

PARIS was born on a little island in the Seine that has been known for many centuries as the Ile de la Cité (the island of the city). On it stands the famous medieval Cathedral of Notre Dame. Across from the island, on the left bank of the Seine, is a low hill whose slopes have been known for centuries as the Latin Quarter. Here in the Middle Ages students debated all kinds of questions in Latin. Here grew up the most famous university in the world, the University of Paris, whose liberal arts college is now called the Sorbonne. Today, thousands of students still debate the greatest questions of human existence in the same Latin Quarter.

The students no longer debate in Latin. They debate in French, in German, in English, in nearly all the living languages of the world. For here, in the Latin Quarter, one of the great French industries is carried on. The invention, the clarification and the marketing of ideas is as much a great industry of Paris as is the dressing of women or the manufacture of jewelry. The cafés of the Latin Quarter are the direct descendants of the inns and drinking houses where the medieval students debated and often fought. And the French are fully conscious of the continuity of this history. Most of the great European debates have either begun in Paris or have been given universal form there. And many of the strong points and weak points in French intellectual habits were shaped many hundreds of years ago in Paris.

TO begin with, the French language was formed in Paris, formed not only by the students and teachers of the university, but by the lawyers of the king's courts, by the merchants, by the nobles. By the 15th Century the language we know today was readily identifiable as such and had already acquired many of its greatest virtues. It was already clear and systematic. Already its users delighted in argument and in verbal elegance.

It is this continuity of culture, unequaled in any other European country, that has so colored the French mind. In the postwar years, for example, the most fashionable and possibly the most important philosophical doctrine in the western world was existentialism. Not only did this complicated creed find its clearest exposition in Paris, but Frenchmen in discussing it were likely to recall such remote controversies as those which took place in the 12th Century between St. Bernard, one of the very greatest of medieval saints, and Abélard, the first of the internationally famous Paris professors. It is not un-French that Abélard should be even more famous for his dramatic love affair with Héloïse. In every age since the 12th Century Frenchmen have been delighting or scandalizing Europe with their ideas and their conduct.

Often these Frenchmen have been bitterly opposed to each other. It has never been safe in any century to talk simply of "the French mind," for there have always been minority voices. Thus in the 17th Century, when the French language was given its classical form and when there were impressive orthodox doctrines in church and state, in literature and science,

there were also dissenting voices. The mathematical genius Blaise Pascal turned away from mathematics and physics to religion, and from knowledge of the world to the problem of salvation. The greatest French writer of tragedy, Racine, was also deeply preoccupied with the problem of salvation. At the height of his career he gave up writing secular tragedies and for the rest of his life wrote only two plays, both on Biblical topics. The greatest writer of comedy, Molière, was a bitter foe of ecclesiastical hypocrisy and an ambiguous Christian. The greatest literary figure of the 16th Century, Rabelais, was an enemy of many abuses in the Church and an uproarious critic of what he considered decadent Catholic philosophy.

Even in the 18th Century, when the dominating figure was Voltaire, for whom clarity was the supreme intellectual virtue, there was a counterattack preaching the importance of the emotions. And that came from Jean-Jacques Rousseau of Geneva, brought up in the little community that had been ruled by the most rigorous of Protestant theologians, the Frenchman John Calvin. One can put side by side two French sayings. One by Rivarol asserts, "What is not clear is not French." The other, by Pascal, asserts, "The heart has its reasons that reason knows nothing of." Both these truths about the French mind must be remembered.

THERE are other truths to be remembered. First of all France, which intellectually means Paris, is no longer as much the world market for ideas as she was in the 13th Century or the 17th and 18th Centuries. There is, to begin with, a new center of doctrine and discussion in Moscow, a center to which many Frenchmen themselves look for light and leading. Secondly, there are in the western world other centers of learning, like the universities of Great Britain and the United States, which equal Paris in importance and in some fields surpass her. Then, for much more than a century, the French have been taking in ideas as well as giving them out, and until very recent times they have been learning more from Germany than from any other country. All through the 19th and 20th Centuries the main philosophical influences on France have come from Germany. Kant was almost the official philosopher of the Third Republic, and Hegel—straight and in a Marxian version—has been extremely powerful.

It cannot be doubted that the curiosity with which the Frenchman now looks to the outside world for instruction and inspiration reflects his new skepticism about the universal validity of the French way of doing things in the intellectual as well as in the material world. The average Frenchman, not merely the sophisticated and rebellious intellectual, is more ready to be taught by foreign teachers than he was in past ages. But there still survives in France a national "culture" that is unified, organized and accepted to a degree unknown in any other western country.

WHAT is the special mark of French culture? It is a culture giving priority to language and to literary polish. Among living literatures, only English can compete in durability and variety. But at no time in English history has literary proficiency played so great a part as it has in French life. In two other arts, painting and architecture, French achievement is almost as great as in literature. And it could be said that French architecture and much of French painting have many of the qualities of French literature: sobriety, form and elegance.

Be that as it may, it is in their literature that the French recognize themselves best. Ever since the middle of the 17th Century there has been a French literary culture, in prose and in verse, to which all Frenchmen have felt obliged to pay allegiance. Cardinal Richelieu, the great 17th Century prime minister who consolidated the power of the monarchy and severely curbed the feudal lords, also established a literary institution called the French Academy, the purpose of which was to curb anarchy in language and style and to encourage obedience to the rules of good taste. These rules, it was thought, could be set out as a code of laws. And it was not only professional writers who were supposed to obey them, but every educated man and woman.

The result was the creation of a culture admired and imitated all over Europe, even in England. Just as foreign kings imitated the great palace of Louis XIV at Versailles, so also they established academies on the French model, and many of them, like Frederick the Great of Prussia and Catherine the Great of Russia, used French as their habitual language. This "classical" French replaced Latin as the international language and, indeed, has lost its dominant position only in this century. The possession of this international tongue by all educated men and women in Europe, even if their mother tongue was German or Italian or Russian, was a great advantage to France. In many ways it still is. But there were and are drawbacks to this cultural uniformity.

The crystal-clear classical language could not say everything that human beings wanted to say. It could often be pompous and empty. With the coming of what we call the romantic movement in the 19th Century, with the acceptance of the right of emotion to express itself in violent language if necessary, classical French began to lose its unique position. French writers began to look to England and Germany for literary inspiration, and at the very time that the Revolutionary government in the 1790s began to impose French as the sole legal language in the new republic, the old French culture began to split.

THAT split is very evident today and has important social and political consequences. From the point of view of international science and culture, modern French is not nearly so clear and exact a language as the old classical French was. It has had to accept English, Russian, Spanish and German as rival modern languages, and this decline represents more than a mere decline of the French state.

First of all, the imposed unity of the age of Louis XIV has gone. Voltaire was perhaps the most formidable enemy of orthodox Christianity in modern times. He was a powerful influence in places as far apart as Aberdeen and Yale, but it was in the French-speaking countries that his

SACRÉ-COEUR

MONTMARTRE

ARC DE TRIOMPHE

PARC MONCEAU

MADELEINE

OPÉRA

BIBLIOTHÈQUE NATIONALE

CHAMPS-ELYSÉES

PETIT PALAIS

PLACE DE LA CONCORDE

PALAIS ROYALE

THÉÂTRE-FRANÇAIS

MUSEUM OF MODERN ART

GRAND PALAIS

TUILERIES

LOUVRE MUSEUM

EIFFEL TOWER

LEFT

NAPOLEON'S TOMB

BANK

PLACE DES VOSGES

NOTRE DAME

L'INSTITUT

ARSENAL LIBRARY

LEFT BANK BISTRO

to VERSAILLES

SORBONNE

LATIN QUARTER

LUXEMBOURG GARDEN

PASTEUR INSTITUTE

INTELLECTUAL MAP OF PARIS shows where artists, writers and students have long congregated. Authors, musicians and Bohemians haunt the slopes of Montmartre; all three are memorialized in the Parc Monceau and the Place des Vosges. Noted libraries include the Arsenal and the Bibliothèque Nationale. Performing arts are centered at the Opéra and the Théâtre-Français. Serious painters, once a Montmartre fixture, now frequent the Left Bank, many studying at l'Institut and hoping to end up in museums like the Modern or the Louvre. French and foreign students attend the Sorbonne and the Pasteur Institute. Other landmarks are ones familiar in art and in literature.

attacks on Catholic fanaticism had the greatest effect. There are, of course, many other reasons for the present alienation of a great part of the French people from the Catholic Church, particularly its support of right-wing political movements. Whatever the causes, a great part of the French people today are indifferent to the Christian religion and a great part of the French people are hostile to it.

One consequence is that the believing French Catholics are militantly intellectual. They know they have to fight for their faith and cannot rely upon a public opinion which assumes the general rightness of Christianity or even the existence of God. Some of the greatest names of modern French literature have been those of dedicated Catholics like the poet and dramatist (and ambassador) Paul Claudel and the novelist and Nobel laureate François Mauriac.

Two of the most important living French philosophers, Jacques Maritain and Gabriel Marcel, are Catholics. But their religious philosophy is not of a type that the man in the street can easily assimilate. If it reaches him at all, it reaches him percolating through novels, sermons, newspaper and magazine stories and plays (Marcel has the advantage of being a dramatist as well as a philosopher). With these defenders of the faith there is no acceptance of the view that the object of religion is peace of mind or adjustment to this world.

IF a great part of the French people are alienated from the Catholic Church, a still greater part are alienated from bourgeois society—the business class. Here it is necessary to distinguish between the legitimate, if not particularly intelligent, resentment of the French worker at his share in the rewards of the French way of life and the alienation of much of the French bourgeoisie from itself.

This is an old story. All through the 19th Century most French writers were highly critical of the established order. Some were critical from royalist and Catholic points of view, but most were critics who wanted to carry on the work of the Revolution and to "liberate the people."

Two of the greatest figures of the 19th Century, Jules Michelet the historian and Victor Hugo the poet, dramatist and novelist, both adored "the people" and saw themselves as leaders in the people's liberation. Even such recondite poets as Charles Baudelaire and Arthur Rimbaud felt it necessary to take, at one period of their lives, a revolutionary stand.

THE antibourgeois feeling has continued in this century. François Mauriac is not only a militant Catholic but a ruthless critic of the wealthy winegrowing bourgeoisie of the Bordeaux region, to which he belongs. In his novels the philosophical writer Jean-Paul Sartre exposes the sterility and baseness of bourgeois society. So in another sense did the late Albert Camus. The list is nearly endless. Mademoiselle Françoise Sagan is not ostensibly a social or political critic, but the world of her novels is not one to breed admiration for modern French moneyed society.

It is possible to take these critics of society too seriously. Many French people do take them too seriously because of the old tradition that a skilled writer, a masterful manipulator of the French language, must have something of value to say about social questions. Certainly the middle class itself constitutes most of the following of these authors. Even Louis Aragon, the poet and novelist who is the greatest literary ornament of the French Communist party, is not the author that the working-class, rank-and-file Communists most want to read.

For there is another cleavage in French culture, possibly almost as important as the religious cleavage. French literary culture today has become more and more an affair of small groups, of difficult techniques, of highly individual points of view. The great French writers of the past were admired by all ranks of society. The most popular of the French dramatists, Molière, was also one of the greatest. The most popular of French poets, La Fontaine, author of the famous fables, was also one of the greatest. Balzac was as popular a novelist as Dickens and Mark Twain. But the greatest of the *modern*

French poets, from Baudelaire on, have been difficult, perverse and baffling.

The greatest of modern French novelists, Marcel Proust, not only wrote in a style that was novel and not easy but wrote about an extremely restricted section of French society: the upper world of Paris, of dukes and millionaires and famous courtesans. Probably the average Frenchmen and Frenchwomen of all classes still handle their language better than is done in any other country and know their own classics better than is common in either Britain or America. But the fashionable French literature today, so much admired by the sophisticated in London, New York, Chicago, Munich and Stockholm, is not that which is either read or appreciated by the mass of the French people. If, as is often asserted, the young French of today care less for literature than their fathers did, this may be partly because much of the most prestige-laden modern French literature makes no general appeal and is not designed to make one.

THE official sanction of certain writers by the French Academy no longer carries the weight it did. French intellectual leaders assume that few of the best current authors will belong to the French Academy, a view that was in a way confirmed in 1955 when the Academy elected the late Jean Cocteau, for long the *enfant terrible* of the arts in France. Bold experimenter in poetry, drama, ballet and films, Cocteau had been the embodiment of revolt in French culture. And he characteristically justified his entry into the Academy by declaring that since it was the practice of the most fashionable pioneers in literature to condemn the Academy as a mausoleum, the truly original thing to do was to join it.

The Goncourt Academy, an unofficial organization which once a year gives a prize for the best new French novel, has preserved its prestige, but quite often critics and readers are at a loss to decide why a particular book has been crowned. And it is assumed that many thousands of Frenchmen buy the current Goncourt novel to show their intellectual respectability rather than with any firm intention of reading it.

But it would be a mistake to write off the widespread French preoccupation with literature and ideas as mere humbug. Much of the French "educated" population has, at any rate, received elementary training in philosophy. Stating human problems and even political problems in philosophical terms seems natural to the representative Frenchman. Thus a great part of the appeal of Marxism comes from its philosophical background, from its statements about the human situation. Many Frenchmen are Marxists because it is "progressive." Marxism tells them how the world is going and must go and why they should adjust themselves to the inevitable triumph of the workers. Needless to say, the Communist party appeals to the workers in less abstract and intellectual terms, but Marxism gains among educated Frenchmen because it is both a philosophy *and* a political program.

EQUALLY representative of the French approach to public questions was the prestige of existentialism. The origins of existentialism are mainly German, although its most attractive begetter was the noted Danish philosopher and theologian of a century ago, Sören Kierkegaard. However, it was not in its German or Danish but in its French version that existentialism became an important social as well as philosophical doctrine. As a philosophical doctrine it is remote from ordinary ideas and involves the use of a special vocabulary. Again, even the well-educated Frenchman is not concerned mainly with the difference between "essence" and "existence." He wants moral and political leadership, and he will accept that leadership more easily if he feels and, better still, if he understands that it is philosophically respectable. He may get it in a Christian form from Gabriel Marcel or the late Emmanuel Mounier. But the most potent and fashionable form has been the atheistic existentialism of Jean-Paul Sartre.

Sartre is primarily a moralist concerned with man's situation in a universe he finds godless and with man's duty in such a universe. His doctrine, as he himself has insisted rightly, is not a doctrine of despair. His solitary man is called upon to accept total responsibility for his own life. He should be *engagé*—committed to this moral life and not passive in the face of a godless and heedless universe.

BEHIND this doctrine lies a complicated, subtle and, some critics think, inconsistent philosophical theory, but many young people after the 1944 liberation looked to Sartre and his then-ally Albert Camus for positive leadership. They were repelled by tradition, skeptical of religion and fearful of the authoritarianism of the Communist party. Many felt themselves to be in Sartre's dilemma: "If the Party is right I am more lonely than a madman. If the Party is wrong, the world is done for." There *had* to be some way out of this dilemma, and Sartre tried to show the way in novels, plays, tracts and speeches.

Non-Frenchmen may think there is something comic in the belief that so sophisticated a philosophical system could be made the basis, even in a simplified form, of effective political action. And the indifference of Sartre and many of his disciples to the economic problems facing the French worker in the late 1940s gave the Communists an easy chance to score political gains. But it is a fact about France that sophisticated doctrines have a powerful appeal: the split in the early 1950s between Sartre and Camus over Sartre's uncritical defense of the Communists was an important political event. And for some time a great many French intellectuals were reassured by the fact that André Malraux, the eminent soldier, novelist, art critic and propagandist, was one of the closest associates of General De Gaulle.

One of the excitements of life in Paris is this continual exchange of ideas and programs, the liveliness of the controversies and the quickness of the minds. These seem part of the climate of the city. But the foreigner or the critical Frenchman who knows something about the outside world is sometimes struck by the thought that perhaps too much time is spent in cafés, in salons and at public meetings discussing questions which cannot effectually be discussed except in small and specialized groups. True, France—not just Paris—is extremely rich in magazines of discussion, and the French academic tradition puts a high price on lucidity and acuteness. And the old French tradition of admiration for literary finish leads to the presentation of problems in elegant literary forms and the solution of them in equally elegant literary forms. Neither the problems nor the solutions may have much relation to the objective realities of the modern world. Indeed, many Frenchmen seem to think that to state a problem clearly is to answer it.

But there are signs that, for good or ill, the old French preoccupation with verbal discussion does not have the prestige or the primacy it had. There is the competition of other arts, notably music. There is the improved standing of physical science and technology. The country of Voltaire is also the country of Pasteur. The country of dynasties of great mathematicians is also the country of bold, original engineers. In a discussion of social questions, of the role of "the people," much more attention is now paid to American techniques of social investigation and to the application of statistical methods, and less to literary polish. French economists, for long sadly lacking in originality or profundity, are now beginning to make serious contributions in more than one field. The very decline of generally accepted style in novels and plays makes mere "style" less of an asset (and less of an answer to complex problems of this world) than it used to be.

FRANCE is still a country, however, in which the things of the mind have an automatic prestige and the handlers of ideas are taken very seriously. It was as an original military thinker, and as a writer whose style was at least not banal, that the young Charles de Gaulle in the 1930s first attracted the attention—not all of it friendly—of his military superiors. And it is still worth noting that the general's memoirs, written in an admirable version of classical French, are regarded by many of his countrymen today as proof of an additional—and relevant—form of personal greatness.

EXISTENTIALIST Jean-Paul Sartre has influenced an entire generation of writers in both Europe and America. In 1964 he refused to accept the Nobel Prize because he did not wish to become obligated to an institution.

MINISTER OF CULTURAL AFFAIRS André Malraux (*left*) exchanges ideas with Nobel Prize author François Mauriac at a 1965 political gathering in Paris. Malraux is a successful novelist and a renowned expert on art.

An Esteem
for Leaders
of Intellect

In no other country today are the proponents of new ideas esteemed so highly as in France. Coiners of the term *avant-garde*, the French have long encouraged the daring and the experimental in literature and the arts—in recent years most notably in motion pictures. Not infrequently, intellectual leaders are called upon to take high government posts, and philosophical disputes between authors can become political issues.

PHILOSOPHER PRIEST, the late Pierre Teilhard de Chardin tried to reconcile science and religion. His writings have gained international attention since his death in 1955.

OFFBEAT FILMS *conceived
by the imaginative, unregimented
directors of "the new wave"
uphold a great French tradition
of bold and perceptive motion pictures*

DIRECTOR ALAIN RESNAIS, who created the classic *Last Year at Marienbad*, uses technical innovations in a continuing search for the reality that exists beneath all appearance.

SYLVAN STRANGLING, a woodland scene in which the heroine is throttled by her lover, is directed for the movie *Les Bonnes Femmes* by Claude Chabrol (*center, with glasses*).

INNOVATOR Eugene Ionesco satirizes conformity in bizarre plays like *The Rhinoceros*. Born in Romania, he is a star of the Paris literary world.

INDIVIDUALIST, the late Albert Camus aroused an intellectual storm when he broke with Jean-Paul Sartre in 1952. At right he directs a play.

LITERARY REBELS, *always at home in France, wage merciless war on conformity and complacency, on bigotry and political inaction, and above all on the sins they detect among the rich and wellborn*

PRECOCIOUS CRITIC Françoise Sagan amazed the book-buying public when she was 18 with her bitter but well-written 1954 novel, *Bonjour Tristesse*, exposing French bourgeois society. Its huge sales, which enabled her to buy a leopard-skin coat and a sports car (*above*), made her a world-wide symbol of the indignation of adolescence.

LONELY RITES of mass are performed in a café of a village whose church is closed down. The priest is one who took part in an ill-fated revival drive a few years ago.

Challenge to Teachers and Priests

THERE are few countries in Europe in which the national culture is as consciously developed as in France. There is hardly any country in which differences of accent or provincial origin cause less discomfort. The Duchesse de Guermantes, the brilliant social heroine of the greatest of all modern French novels, Marcel Proust's *Remembrance of Things Past*, was proud of her "peasant" accent. And at a Paris wedding a few years ago one of the two cooks concerned was overheard quoting the poet Paul Verlaine to the other. Both of these paradoxes reflect, in part, the cultural unity of France that has been achieved by the inculcation of the idea of a national heritage into generations of French school children. Still more they reflect the success of the First Republic in making standard French the language of all the French people.

The First Republic in 1795 merely laid the foundations of this unified culture, but it laid them well. In its anti-religious fervor the Legislative Assembly had swept away the old medieval *collèges* (private secondary schools run for the most part by ecclesiastics) and the decadent universities. It proposed to replace them with a system of universal public education.

The First Republic's reforms were badly needed. Under the monarchy, the secondary schools run by the religious orders had effectively accomplished their somewhat narrowly conceived task of instructing the sons of the middle and upper classes. But the university system was in an advanced state of decay in 1789. "The Sorbonne," the name then given to the theological faculty of the University of Paris, was outdated and church-ridden, and it suffered by comparison with the contemporary universities of Glasgow and Edinburgh, Göttingen and Leyden, and even with Oxford and Cambridge. The First Republic undertook to renew the whole educational system. The *collèges* were replaced by modern secondary schools organized on a secular basis with a strong scientific bias. The provincial universities were broken up into various degree-granting "faculties," and special schools were created like the Ecole Normale Supérieure, the famous teacher-training school, and the renowned Ecole Polytechnique, the first great technological institution in the world designed to produce engineers and scientifically trained soldiers. (One of the most illustrious children of the Ecole Polytechnique is the U.S. Military Academy at West Point.)

THE First Republic promised more than it performed. Its aim of establishing a democratic system of state schools was frustrated by lack of funds. Later, Napoleon discarded the principle of secular education that the First Republic had adopted when he reinstated most of the teaching privileges of the Church. In 1806 he created an administrative apparatus called "the Imperial University." This was intended to control all aspects of French education from the Church-run elementary schools up through the Ecole Polytechnique and in effect established a national ministry of education.

Napoleon was not very much interested in elementary schools, however. The aim of his system was to provide the government with competent and loyal civil servants and soldiers from the upper class. These would receive excellent training. In the neglected primary schools, however, some of the children of the poor were taught to read and write and little else. Students at every level were instructed to respect the Catholic Church and the emperor.

FRANCE'S changing 19th Century governments, from Napoleon to the founding of the Third Republic in 1870, made various efforts to improve French education. A national system of primary instruction was organized in 1833, but serious education remained an affair for the male children of the upper and middle classes. They were taught in state *lycées* (high schools with very high academic standards), in the provincial "faculties" and in the *grandes écoles* (the national higher professional schools). The education of the peasants and the workers was left to ill-paid schoolmasters or to members of religious brotherhoods in Church schools. (The secular primary schools were of a much lower caliber than the Church-run institutions.) The girls of the middle and upper classes, if they were educated at all, were sent to convent schools, whose object was to make good Catholic mothers of them rather than to give them any kind of advanced education.

The French educational system thus catered at three different levels to three different groups of French people: the boys of well-to-do families in the *lycées*, the girls of the same families in the convents, and the great mass of ordinary French people in the primary schools. There was even a fourth sector, for to an increasing degree the male children of the more prosperous classes were sent to schools run by religious orders like the Jesuits and the Dominicans, who with notable success competed with the state *lycées*. This system gave France a cultivated and intellectually conceited elite. But it did not have a democratic basis, and it was not intended to have one.

With the coming of the Third Republic in 1870 the old order was put on the defensive. It was the mark of a good republican to be a friend of the schools, and many laws were passed in the next few decades to promote popular education. Religious instruction in state-supported schools was abolished in 1881 and the national educational system became entirely secular. Secondary schools for girls were created by the government at this time.

It would be foolish to underestimate the success of the Third Republic's educational system. By 1900 France was equipped everywhere with adequate elementary schools taught by competent, if narrow-minded and limited, teachers. And the state *lycées* offered an excellent and relatively inexpensive, if old-fashioned, education which benefited a great many children of the lower middle class.

The Third Republic also re-created the provincial universities, uniting the separate faculties of law, letters, medicine and science into establishments with local ties. The University of Paris was expanded, and its name became as glorious as it had been in the Middle Ages. Nevertheless, the great mass of the French people were still excluded from higher education. The system was not only far less democratic than the American one but even less democratic than the new English system of primary and secondary schools.

THE catastrophe of World War I did not seriously alter the French educational system. It did, however, reduce the tension between church and state. Religious orders that had been expelled were allowed to come back quietly. There were now many lay Catholic teachers at every level of the state educational system. The general rise in the intellectual repute of French Catholics that had begun in the second half of the 19th Century was now reflected not only in the improved status of the tuition-free Catholic universities, of which the Institut Catholique in Paris was the most famous, but in the increasing number of state university professors who were loyal both to the Republic and to the Church.

Between the two wars there were repeated demands that the school system be democratized, but the few timid steps made in that direction were utterly inadequate. The system remained undemocratic—it was almost impossible for a member of the lower classes to progress beyond the public primary schools—and now it was out of date. As one authority has pointed out, the educational system was not capitalist but precapitalist. Its ideal was the *honnête homme* (well-rounded gentleman) of the 17th Century, a man whose literary culture was the fruit of abundant leisure. It was not designed to produce businessmen or to increase the national income. Although France during the first half of the 19th Century had been one of the great pioneers in all forms of science, medicine and technology, after 1870 she had fallen behind Germany and even England in the utilization of science for industrial purposes. So with the end of World War II the French educational system was scrutinized much as the economic system was examined in the light of the disaster of 1940.

THE Fourth Republic undertook to fulfill the promises of the Third Republic, to give all French boys and girls the opportunity for an advanced modern education and to give the nation an educational system adapted to the 20th Century instead of the 17th. But the promises were hard to keep. A shortage of schoolrooms was made much more serious by the sudden rise in the birth rate, and there was a shortage of teachers at all levels. The repeated devaluation of the franc in the late 1940s impoverished the teaching profession. France needed more teaching of science and technology and both these disciplines demanded highly expensive equipment. Educational experts remarked that the money which should have provided adequate schools was being poured down the "rat holes" of Indochina and Algeria.

Much of the French people's criticism of their educational system arises from the intense seriousness with which they approach the subject. To an American, the fact that at every stage of the elaborate examination system many pupils fail implies that the educational system is not succeeding. To the French it proves that the system is succeeding. The object of the system is to separate the bright pupils from the not-so-bright ones, and it does so, revealing the fact that a great many people, even in France, are either lazy or stupid, which is not news to the French. Undoubtedly the high school baccalaureate examination, familiarly called the *bachot*, is too severe, and some efforts are now being made to liberalize it. In any event, the fact that André Gide and Françoise Sagan both failed in their first attempts to pass the *bachot* does not really shock the French people very much.

A more reasonable argument against the system is that it puts too much emphasis on easily recognizable intellectual qualities, especially on facility in handling the French language and in expressing abstract ideas. The examinations for entrance into the *grandes écoles* are savagely competitive, and so are the examinations at the end of the courses. Perhaps too many intelligent French boys and girls are exhausted by this type of competition, but at least the result is that those who get over these hurdles have been tested seriously on their ability to master difficult subjects.

EVEN the French themselves are beginning to admit that the traditional French culture is not wholly relevant to the modern world. For example, French institutions of higher learning graduate about 4,000 engineers a year. Those who come from the Ecole Polytechnique and other centers of technical education are very well trained, but there are not enough of them. And the class bias in French education keeps many thousands of ingenious boys and girls from attending good technical schools—boys and girls who in America (or even in England) would be given a training, not indeed as elaborate as is given in the Ecole Polytechnique, but adequate for the needs of modern industry.

It is not only a question of the shortage of teachers and institutions. It is a question of the bias of a system which produces far too many lawyers, far too many people with literary skills

and possibly even too many doctors, but not nearly enough engineers, physicists or chemists.

Proposals to divert talented French boys and girls from the humanities to science and technology invariably evoke protests from the traditionalists. But the economic facts of life are defeating the traditionalists. An engineer can always get a well-paid job, while a graduate in philosophy or literature may have no alternative to entering the badly paid state school system or becoming a publisher's hack. What the traditionalists criticize as "Americanization" is as potent in the educational world as in industry. It is a part of the adjustment that France is having to make to her new situation as an industrial power of the first rank. Recent reforms have been aimed at broadening the country's educational base.

One of the bitterest quarrels in contemporary France since the establishment of the Fifth Republic has concerned Church schools. Marshal Pétain's wartime regime had instituted subsidies for Church schools, but these were abolished in 1945. Today a fifth of all French children go to Church schools, and in some western areas such as Normandy and Brittany, which are predominantly Catholic, practically all the children do. Most of the Catholic schools are necessarily short of money for paying the teachers and maintaining the buildings. If the Church were to abandon these institutions (and some Catholics think this would be the wisest solution) the state schools would be flooded with children whom they could not accommodate.

IT was natural, therefore, for the Fourth Republic to reinstate subsidies to the Church schools in a minor way. And it was natural for the Fifth Republic to subsidize them more openly. Yet the debate which preceded this reasonable compromise evoked the most violent passions on both sides. In the eyes of the Left any subsidy was treason, and Socialists and Radicals joined the Communists in opposing it. On the other hand, zealous Catholics, while willing to take the state's money, were unwilling to allow any state control of Church schools. In the political torpor of the Fifth Republic it was this question, to an outsider not one of the first importance, that for a time excited most Frenchmen in discussions of domestic politics.

The quarrel is in every sense characteristically French. It is a quarrel about the nature of the French state and the French nation. For centuries France has been referred to as "the eldest daughter of the Church." The First Republic saw France as the liberating instrument of progress, and its vision of progress included the death, violent or natural, of Catholic institutions. Even though the old bitterness of the church-and-state quarrel has diminished, the issue remains. Is France a Catholic country?

IN many parts of France there is as much need to preach Christianity as there is in any missionary territory. This is true not only of the industrial regions but of many parts of the countryside where in the course of the last century Christianity has simply evaporated. Often the village church is closed down, and even when it is open the priest may have only a handful of the faithful to support him in an almost unbearably lonely and unrewarding task. While there are some active Catholics in a few industrial areas, they are a conspicuous minority.

It was the realization of this fact that led some years ago to the experiment of the "worker priests," who, it was hoped, would gain access to the non-Christian masses by working alongside them. The plan failed at first. Some of the worker priests became Communists, while some married and refused to obey the Vatican when it bade them return to normal clerical life. Now the experiment is being retried, with safeguards.

But if the Catholic Church in France has to fight against active hostility as well as mere indifference, it is a highly combative and in many ways very competent organization. France is still the greatest Catholic missionary country in the world. Although she is a much less ardently Catholic country than West Germany, she produces far more priests. The greatest ornaments of the international religious orders are usually Frenchmen. To Catholics the world over,

the most popular of all modern saints is Teresa of Lisieux, "the Little Flower," who was French. The most popular religious shrine in the world is at Lourdes in southern France. The most impressive contemporary application of the fine arts to religious purposes is in France, by painters like Rouault and Matisse; the most famous modern Catholic thinker was the Jesuit Teilhard de Chardin.

To the representative Frenchman, religion means Catholicism—in the sense that most families still go through the formality of baptizing their children in the Church. Yet both Protestants and Jews play a very important part in French national life. The failure of the Protestant Reformation to conquer France was one of the most important events in both French and European history. The French Protestants lost out, but they became and have remained a very important minority. Odiously persecuted under Louis XIV, many of them emigrated to other countries, and in all the countries to which they moved they rose to the top in scholarship, business, politics and war. But many of them stayed in France, and some built large French industries. The most prominent families make up what is referred to as the "H.S.P." (the Haute Société Protestante), the Protestant upper class which has intermarried, interbred, run many of the banks and had a political and social influence quite out of proportion to its numbers.

AMONG the French Protestants two major groups must be distinguished. There are the members of the Reformed Church, once rigorous Calvinists but now very like American Presbyterians, and there are the Lutherans of Alsatian origin. Of these Lutherans the most famous is the late missionary doctor, Albert Schweitzer, whose nephew, Pierre-Paul Schweitzer, is now director of the International Monetary Fund. Another Alsatian Protestant is Wilfrid Baumgartner, long-time head of the Bank of France and for two years De Gaulle's Minister of Finance.

The Reformed Protestants are as active in business as Lutherans. Thus, the great Peugeot automobile dynasty is Reformed. But Protestants share with the Catholics the problem of the general indifference of the French to religion. In some Protestant villages in the South the minister has as hard a time as the priest in nominally Catholic villages. The peasants are Protestant only in the sense that they are not Catholic. And if active Catholics in the great urban centers are a small minority, active Protestants are almost unknown.

In some ways the position of the French Jews is like that of the Protestants. There are some very old Jewish communities in France that go back many hundreds of years. These communities are mainly located in the South, and the most important descendant of this group is the former premier, Pierre Mendès-France. Another section of the modern French Jewish population comes from Alsace, and its most outstanding representative was the late Léon Blum, for long the leader of the Socialist party. A third group is composed of immigrants from eastern Europe. The most famous of modern French philosophers, Henri Bergson, was a child of this immigration, and although he had intellectually been converted to Catholicism before he died in 1941, he refused to claim exemption from the anti-Jewish laws of the Pétain regime.

LIKE the Protestants, the Jews of France are prominent in business and industry, notably in banking (the Paris branch of the world-famous Rothschild family is still powerful in French finance). They are also well represented in academic circles, and one of the greatest modern French novelists, Marcel Proust, was half Jewish. Although anti-Semitism has played a part in modern French life, it is now mostly associated with the humiliations of the regime of Marshal Pétain. President de Gaulle's finance minister, Michel Debré, is the grandson of a rabbi. The flood of Jewish refugees from Algeria, however, has put a great strain on the charity of the French Jewish community.

Despite the quarrels over Church schools, despite the alienation of the mass of the French people from Christianity, France is less divided today by religious quarrels than at any time since the Reformation. This is no doubt partly due to mere indifference. But it is due also to the realization that the sectarian divisions of France are a source of national weakness and often the cause of national disgrace.

UP until the 20th Century French Catholics dreamed of a country restored to unity through the Church. Republicans dreamed of a "republic one and indivisible" in which the Church would gradually wither away and national unity would be formed around a new lay ideal. Neither of these great opposing parties now hopes for the disappearance of the other. Even the Communists do not really expect France to be transformed into an effective Soviet satellite. All sides are deeply French in their passionate conviction that truth matters and that a man's philosophy of life is as important as his day-to-day practice of it.

The French in the Middle Ages arrogantly described the Crusades as *gesta Dei per Francos* (deeds of God done by the French). Even an atheist philosopher like Jean-Paul Sartre is convinced that France must be a moral and intellectual leader, that she must be "engaged" in the struggle for a new world. The active French Catholics—a minority, but a militant, highly organized and intelligent minority—are convinced that in the battle to shape the modern world the French Church must be, as in the past, a leader, perhaps *the* leader. French Protestants and Jews are convinced that they have *their* contribution to give. And France, though not a nation of churchgoers, is perhaps the country where religion is debated with more passion, intelligence and conviction than anywhere else in the world.

Religious and anti-religious parties in France may not yet love each other, but they hate each other less than they did. They are even willing to admit that the other side may have something to contribute, if only because it keeps them in a high state of intellectual and moral training. The old and ruinous antagonism is not yet dead, but it is dying.

Ambling gaily along an upland road amid the snow-clad mountains of Auvergne, four children make their way home from school.

Schooling: Classical and Tough

French educators have summed up the difference between schools in France and in America by saying that while the U.S. tries to create the citizen, France tries to educate the man. The classics-oriented schooling is tough. Intellectual achievement is universally appreciated, and teachers are respected members of the community. Many children start in nursery school at the age of two, although education is compulsory only between six and 16. Competition for scholarships is stiff, for good jobs in the centralized civil service go to those with top scholastic records.

119

EDUCATION FOR ALL *is a continuing government goal.*
But while one fifth of the national budget goes for schools, funds are still
inadequate, and the shortcomings produce occasional public outcries

SITTING TO PROTEST, 2,000 university students in Paris park themselves on the Rue Sufflot pavement near the famed Pantheon (*background*). Their object was to persuade the government not to reduce their social security funds, which pay for tuberculosis treatment. The government refused and the students went back to class.

RISING TO RECITE, a beaming girl takes part in class-room work at a school in St.-Germain-en-Laye, near Paris. Primary studies (except for instruction in music and art) are uniform throughout France, and most classes are run strictly. Parents must sign children's homework to show they are aware of the work the children are doing.

CARRYING CANDLES protected from the wind by paper shields, pilgrims at Lourdes take part in 1958 ceremonies marking the 100th anniversary of the vision of Bernadette.

Hundreds of thousands of sick and crippled come each year to drink and bathe in the waters of the grotto before which young Bernadette heard the voice of the Virgin.

FLOCKING TO THE SHRINE (*right*), pilgrims make their way from the town of Lourdes (*top*) toward the shrine's basilicas (*foreground*) and to the famed grotto beyond.

FABULOUS ERA of French painting is recalled by Henri de Toulouse-Lautrec's 1892 work *At the Moulin Rouge*. The artist appears below the man in the background.

Creator
and Arbiter
of Taste

"GOOD Americans, when they die, go to Paris." This famous remark, made by the great 19th Century Boston wit, Tom Appleton, expressed the truth not only about Americans but about Europeans too, for since the middle of the 17th Century Paris has been a lodestar for tourists. Her inventions in every kind of fashion have been studied on the spot, copied at a distance, travestied and parodied, but never ignored. The French, above all the Parisians, have been the creators and arbiters of taste—the "taste-makers"—for the western world since the days of Louis XIV.

That splendid monarch was himself a work of art and a maker of taste. His clothes, his palaces, his painters, his poets and his musicians were imitated and plagiarized in every civilized country of the West. What the king wore, what his mistresses wore, was news. And so it has been ever since. To be sure, many "French"

125

taste-makers have not been French. Louis XIV's fashionable musician, Jean Baptiste Lully, for example, was a Florentine. Then as now one of the roles of Paris has been to put the final seal of approval on an artistic reputation, whether made by a Frenchman or a non-Frenchman, in Paris herself or abroad.

There have been rebellions against Paris' role of taste arbiter. Toward the end of the 18th Century, London began to set men's fashions, especially for outdoor wear, and it has held the role ever since. Able designers of women's fashions in London, New York, Rome and even Dublin have made gallant attempts to vie with Paris, but so far these attempts have not yet overthrown the leadership of the French.

ONE explanation of the superiority of Paris is simply that she has been in the business so long. This has meant the creation of traditions of workmanship in the luxury trades which cannot be matched in any other city. There are equally good dressmakers, cabinet makers, jewelers and hairdressers in other cities. But there are not so many of them, and in no other city has the development of these minor arts been pursued to such a degree of refinement and perfection. In no other city does there exist such a world devoted to what the novelist Emile Zola called "the happiness of women." Here, as the heroine of *Gentlemen Prefer Blondes* remarked, are "all those historical names . . . like Van Cleef and Arpels. . . ." The history of women's fashion could almost be told in the names of the great Paris dressmakers, starting with Rose Bertin, who dressed Marie Antoinette, and coming down to Hubert de Givenchy, whose salon in recent years has enjoyed the custom of Mrs. John F. Kennedy. In the 19th Century, Charles Frederick Worth, the English couturier, and the Empress Eugénie, Spanish wife of Emperor Napoleon III, managed between them to put women into and out of crinolines in the space of 20 years; but neither could have done it, notwithstanding Worth's talents and the empress's beauty, if they had been in London and Madrid instead of Paris.

Another reason for the long dominance of Paris in the taste-making world has been the fascination foreign visitors have felt for the city. This has brought to Paris, century after century, wealthy foreigners who have spent the revenues from estates in Ireland or Russia on *articles de Paris*—including the women of Paris. Almost 100 years ago, Henry Adams of Boston brought his bride to Paris to be dressed properly, and today there are Englishwomen who feel that one of the handicaps suffered by the Queen of England is that to be patriotic she cannot be dressed outside of London.

Fashion in the large sense, of course, means much more than clothes or even jewelry or perfume. It means works of art of all kinds, ranging from splendid châteaux to fine—or at any rate fashionable—paintings and pieces of sculpture. It means furniture and motor cars. It means new art forms like Diaghilev's Ballets Russes, which was launched from a Paris stage in 1909 like a new missile. It means the world in which the young German poet, Rainer Maria Rilke, was the private secretary of the famous sculptor, Auguste Rodin; where Sylvia Beach, a courageous young American woman, made possible the writing of *Ulysses* by encouraging James Joyce and undertaking to publish the completed book; and where in the 1930s Joyce's fellow Dubliner, Samuel Beckett, served the great man as secretary before going on much later to write his now famous, if cryptic, play *Waiting for Godot*. It is a city to which the whole world wants to come to be amused, to be enlightened, but above all to be in fashion.

THERE are, however, drawbacks to being the capital of fashion and a city of taste-makers. Mere fashion plays too great a part in Parisian life. The reputations of artists, dressmakers and even cooks go up like rockets and down like sticks. Nothing is worse than to be found admiring a fashion too late. Today in Paris many of the bright young French people are busily keeping abreast of what they believe are the latest American and English fads in food, drink and especially popular music.

The most rapidly fluctuating segment of the Paris taste market is what the French call *la haute couture*—"high dressmaking," or high fashion. In order to stay healthy this industry must always change. Twice a year new "collections" must be shown, to be sold and often—despite the elaborate precautions taken—to be copied (or pirated) from Texas to Australia. And each collection is, for the house launching it, like a decisive game in the World Series. Experts and merely passionate spectators are constantly bewildered by the rise and fall of the great houses. Fame, in this highly competitive industry, is often transient, "a garland briefer than a girl's."

AT present there are about 20 major dress houses, the most famous of which include Balenciaga, Dior, Chanel, Cardin, Ricci, Heim, Grès, St.-Laurent, Balmain and Lanvin. Of these only two, Chanel and Lanvin, go back to World War I. The great names of the past—Worth, Paquin, Poiret—are but dimly remembered today. It is mainly a man's trade now and often a young man's trade. Yves Saint-Laurent, for example, was chief designer of the House of Dior at 21.

The total business done by *la haute couture* is not outwardly impressive in terms of money: the dressmaking revenue of all the leading houses never adds up to more than about $25 million a year. But the indirect results of Paris' role as the center of fashion are considerable. They justify the French government's imposing a tax on textiles in order to subsidize *la haute couture*. Very few of the *couture* houses, however, pay their way by selling dresses alone. It is the auxiliary sales of perfumes, accessories, shoes and the like that make them solvent.

A great house such as Dior may have an "angel" like Marcel Boussac, the eminently successful textile magnate (and race horse owner), who provided $500,000 in working capital to get it started. A house's main sales may be made not to individuals but to big American department stores which reproduce the original models on a lavish scale. Many sales are also still made, of course, to women of affluence who want the pleasure of a Paris exclusive.

Like many other artists in Paris, the leading clothes designers are not necessarily French. Balenciaga, a Spaniard, is generally regarded as the world's greatest designer. Captain Edward Molyneux is an Irishman. What is significant is that such artists have to exercise their genius in Paris, because, as Pierre Balmain remarked, the rich artistic tradition of Paris provides a backdrop against which sensitive men can work.

Most Frenchwomen, to be sure, never get near the major houses. Those who know how to dress well have their own "little dressmaker around the corner,"'who does almost as well as the Big 20. There are scores of houses on the fringe of *la haute couture*. After World War II Frenchwomen began learning about the excellent ready-made dresses and suits that were to be found in London and New York, and they created a market for good French ready-mades that sustains many second-echelon dress houses. Today even the great houses make and sell ready-mades, and many of the new, young designers aim directly at the ready-made market.

The influence of the Paris dressmaking houses percolates down to all levels of French feminine society. It even percolates overseas to economically depressed areas in remote countries like Ireland, where peasant girls follow Paris fashions as assiduously and faithfully as they can, despite the preachments of moralists, and where Chanel No. 5 perfume can be bought in the Gaelic-speaking villages of Connemara.

IN the fine arts as such the French have been makers of taste for nearly a thousand years. The two great architectural schools of the Middle Ages, Romanesque (which the English call Norman) and Gothic, are superbly represented in France, and it was there that Gothic had its first and most perfect flowering. Gothic itself was a term of deprecation devised by Italian Renaissance scholars for what was known in the Middle Ages simply as "the French style" —a style that spread from France to England and Ireland, to Germany, Poland and Hungary. Its most notable expression is in the magnificent Cathedral of Chartres, which has the reputation of being the most beautiful example of Gothic in the world. The statuary and stained glass of Chartres, like those of the Cathedral of St. Stephen at Bourges, are among the finest achievements of the western world.

FRANCE's dominance in painting, however, is a relatively recent phenomenon. Only a small number of French artists were of the first rank before the 19th Century: Jean Fouquet and the little-known "Maître de Moulins" in the late 15th Century, the Clouet family in the 16th, Claude Lorrain, Nicolas Poussin and Georges de la Tour in the 17th and François Boucher, Jacques-Louis David, Jean-Honoré Fragonard and Antoine Watteau in the 18th. They were all noteworthy painters, but there were equally illustrious artists in other lands. Then quite suddenly a century ago Paris became the center of the world's visual arts. Since that time nearly every important art movement has started in Paris and few artists have received world-wide acclaim if Paris has not accepted them.

Beginning with Eugène Delacroix, who was the illegitimate son of the famous French diplomat Prince Talleyrand, most of the noted artists of the modern world have produced their greatest works in France, and for the most part in and around Paris. Not all of them have been French. The Italian Amadeo Modigliani, the Spaniard Pablo Picasso and the Russian Marc Chagall have been among the greatest ornaments of the Parisian art world which dominated painting for so many decades. But before them, the originators of the movements that evolved into modern painting were French. Edouard Manet, Claude Monet, Georges Seurat, Paul Gauguin, Henri de Toulouse-Lautrec, Edgar Degas and the well-to-do, opinionated Paul Cézanne (who is almost universally believed to be the most illustrious and influential of modern painters) —all were Frenchmen. So was Henri Matisse, usually considered the only rival in modern times to Picasso.

It must be admitted that the role of Paris as a taste-maker has not been uniformly beneficent. Many French painters whose works were once sought after by the rich and the great are now regarded as having been overrated. Jean-Louis Ernest Meissonier, Edouard Detaille and William Bouguereau were among the most famous painters in the world 80 or 90 years ago, and they are now generally ignored (although there has recently been something of a new vogue for the "quaintness" of Bouguereau). Galleries all over the world are full of works by artists of this type, for Paris excelled in promoting all art, even the mediocre. From every country in the world during the 19th Century students came to study in the Paris art schools, which continued to teach the classical style of painting without paying the slightest attention to artists like Auguste Renoir and Cézanne and the other impressionists and post-impressionists, who were at that time bringing a profound revolution to art.

NOT only was Paris hospitable to artists of all kinds, but in the 19th Century she became the international center of the art business itself. Like so many stock exchange specialists, the Paris art dealers made markets in painters, and Paris became as much a center of fashion in art as of fashion in women's clothes. Today Paris suffers in comparison with London, because the English tax system makes selling pictures more profitable there than in Paris. Nevertheless, it is Paris that sets the fashions which are reflected in London—and in New York as well. To Paris come both the private collectors and the dealers from England, the United States and Germany.

This century-old tradition is exploited very adroitly by the Paris taste-makers. Even rough sketches by painters like Picasso and Matisse have fetched fantastically high prices. And there has always been the problem of outright forgery. The old joke, "Corot painted 2,000 pictures, of which 10,000 are in the United States," reflects something of the artificial character of many Paris art values.

It is possible that French leadership in the visual arts is seriously threatened. Many of the most recent movements have their center in New York and if they do not turn out to be ephemeral, they may represent a decline in the position of Paris. And the higher prices which some of the latest art forms fetch in New York and, indeed, in Paris may be ominous for the traditional role of that city.

It would be an illusion—and an expensive one at that—to imagine that all *articles de Paris* —paintings or dresses, sculpture or jewelry— would prove good investments. Not all Frenchmen have good artistic and cultural taste, and in any French provincial town the horrified visitor can see on sale, and at high prices, pieces of preposterous porcelain, atrociously ugly clocks and even more atrociously ugly furniture. And there is quite a big Paris business in producing these regrettable *objets d'art* for unsophisticated audiences in France. The tides of Paris fashion in the arts often take long to reach the provinces.

AND although France is the home of the small independent craftsman, she is not necessarily the home of satisfactory workmanship when this involves the needs of modern life. Of course discipline has to be imposed rigorously in the great automated factories, as it is in the rapid and always punctual railroad system. But many Frenchmen do not take kindly to such regulations, preferring to work in small independent craftsmen's workshops. The mere thought of keeping regular factory hours and doing only a tiny fragment of some mechanical process is repellent to them. Many of the small workshops produce admirably crafted goods. But a good many do not, for even the best-trained artisans frequently lack the technical resources to compete with modern industry. The truth is that an article made by machine is often better than one made by hand—reluctant though the French are to admit this.

Then there is that important aspect of French life which the French call *le système D*. This is an almost untranslatable phrase for an attitude which is nearly a way of life. The "D" of the system stands for the verb *se débrouiller*, which literally means "to be resourceful," but which has taken on the additional meaning of "cutting your corners fine." A great many Frenchmen take special delight in doing things "out of channels," in arriving at their destination by a slightly irregular route. And in an activity like the making and marketing of works of art and objects of luxury the *système D* can play—and some claim does play—too great a part.

IN only one major art, music, has Paris not been the world's undisputed taste-maker. Until the end of the 19th Century, Paris and France were importers rather than innovators of music. The most important "French" musician of the 17th Century was the Florentine Lully, while in the 18th the most noted "French" musician was the German, Christoph Gluck. François Couperin and Jean Philippe Rameau were outstanding composers of the early 18th Century, but more important progress in music was being made in other countries.

THE TOP 10 FRENCH DAILY PAPERS

France-Soir, Paris	p.m., moderate	1,257,000
Le Parisien Libéré, Paris	a.m., independent-rightist	915,000
Ouest-France, Rennes	a.m., M.R.P. party	663,000
Dauphiné Libéré, Grenoble	a.m., independent	522,000
Le Figaro, Paris	a.m., conservative	501,000
L'Aurore, Paris	a.m., rightist	426,000
La Voix du Nord, Lille	a.m., moderate	417,000
Le Progrès de Lyon, Lyons	a.m. & p.m., leftist	392,000
Sud-Ouest, Bordeaux	a.m., moderate	389,000
Dépêche du Midi, Toulouse	a.m., Radical-Socialist	324,000

CIRCULATION LEADERS of the French daily press are listed at left, with the editorial slant of each paper. The prestigious and independent *Le Monde*, widely read by men in business and government, outranks the top 10 in political influence.

Yet one of the first modern symphony orchestras was that of the Paris Conservatory, and in Hector Berlioz, France produced one of the most influential pioneers of 19th Century music —even if Berlioz was more appreciated in Germany and Russia than in his own country. Berlioz' rich, romantic compositions established him as a rival of Germany's Richard Wagner, even though his music did not become stylish until long after his death.

ANOTHER profound influence was Claude Debussy. The surprising and subtle tonal effects of such compositions as Debussy's tone poem *Prélude à l'Après-midi d'un Faune* (*Prelude to the Afternoon of a Faun*, 1892) and his opera *Pelléas et Mélisande* (1902) started a revolution in music comparable to the one brought about in painting by the impressionists. In fact, Debussy is generally considered the originator of impressionism in music. With the ascendancy of Debussy the importance of Germany began to decrease and Paris became the center of the new movement in music. The Paris Opéra, more imposing as a building than as a musical institution, has long represented the homage of the French state to the art of music, but it was the state's second (and less austere) house, the Opéra Comique, which in 1875 presented the most notable French contribution to lyric opera, Georges Bizet's *Carmen*.

As in so many other things, postwar France has undergone a rejuvenation in music. There are now some first-class music festivals in the provinces—serious music at Besançon, Aix-en-Provence and Prades, and jazz festivals at Juan-les-Pins and Antibes. The discipline of the Paris orchestras has been improved since the war, and the Opéra has been dusted off by De Gaulle's Minister of Cultural Affairs, André Malraux. The French radio organization is an enlightened patron of music, and there is no musical novelty today which does not find a welcome in Paris. The practitioners of the 12-tone scale are well represented. So are pioneers like Pierre Boulez, one of the 12-tone group, whose experiments with *musique concrète* involve a bold use of tape recordings blended together to create weird patterns of sound. Nevertheless, Paris is not a capital in music as it is in the other arts.

In the cultivation and exploitation of taste the French press plays a very important role. Before World War II there were two Parisian dailies with circulations over a million, *Le Petit Parisien* and *Le Journal*. Today only one, *France-Soir*, sells that many copies. But all French newspapers, like the important regional paper *Dépêche du Midi* and the influential *Le Figaro* and *Le Monde*, give ample space to cultural events. Elections to the French Academy, the gossip of the Cannes Film Festival and the awarding of the great literary prizes are all first-class news stories as much as is the Tour de France.

French weeklies, fortnightlies and monthlies play a more important taste-forming role than do their American or English equivalents. From the old and respectable *Revue des Deux Mondes* to the usually well-informed satirical weekly *Le Canard Enchaîné*, the French press devotes a great deal of attention to the cultural world and to the scandals and intrigues associated with it. Books, plays and musical shows are given wide coverage. So are controversies about the present state of the French language, including ineffectual protests against "Franglais" —the incorporation of English and American words. Some of the most learned critics of American jazz are in France. When an American musical has a successful run in one of the big theaters of Paris, that too is important news.

EVEN while it is catering directly to popular taste, the French press believes that nothing should be alien to it, especially not the things of the mind. The great German poet Goethe was an avid reader of *Le Globe*, not because it gave him news of French politics but because it told him about French intellectual movements. Today a good murder or a great sporting event will crowd academic news off French front pages, but it will not crowd it out altogether. And the French press, daily, weekly and monthly, helps to create the atmosphere in which Paris remains the home of all fashion.

After a morning of making ceramics, Russian-born painter Marc Chagall stops at a fountain in the town of Vence to scrub his fingers.

Brilliant Century of Daring

For more than a century the bold innovations of Paris painters dominated art history, starting with impressionism and going on to later movements like cubism, abstract art and expressionism. Some of the artists of this era painted outside Paris: the moody Dutchman Vincent Van Gogh did his most notable canvases in Provence, and the romantic Paul Gauguin won fame for his South Seas works. Today the last of the great men like Chagall (*above*) also live outside the capital, and major new talents are few. But a century's brilliance has left its mark (*following pages*).

THE IMPRESSIONISTS,

whose style involved using light itself to capture reality, began to change painting concepts a century ago. A number of artists used the new method to achieve widely differing effects

GEORGES SEURAT, who painted gay, delicate scenes (*opposite*), was outwardly shy. This portrait is by E. Laurent.

PAUL CEZANNE, shown sitting in the garden of his white-bearded artist friend Camille Pissarro, influenced art with canvases like that opposite.

NEW TECHNIQUE was used in works like *Bridge at Courbevoie* (*left*) by Georges Seurat, who placed myriad dots of color on the canvas, incorporating modern theories of color and optics.

NEW PERSPECTIVE, in which objects are shown as a series of planes, was adopted by Cézanne in many canvases like those of the Montagne Ste.-Victoire (*below*). His style led to cubism.

JEAN ARP (*opposite*), a pioneer in free-form sculpture and a founder of the onetime Dada or nonsensical art movement, polishes a new work in his garden near Paris.

GEORGES BRAQUE, who with Picasso developed cubism, later turned to quiet still lifes, which he painted until his death in 1963. He is shown here at work in his Paris studio.

MODERN MASTERS, *who rebelled against conventional painting in the early 1900s and went on to dominate the art world for half a century, are now old or gone. But the artistic tumult they instigated is still raging*

RAOUL DUFY, famed for his gay water colors of French scenes, paints from an armchair in 1949 while visiting hot springs in Spain. An arthritic, Dufy died in 1953.

135

HENRI MATISSE sits in the gleaming chapel he designed in Vence. It was widely considered his finest work, but Matisse, who died in 1954, was above all known for paintings of sumptuous nudes.

PABLO PICASSO (*opposite*), the most controversial artist of his day, is a Spaniard who has lived many years in France. This portrait by Gjon Mili evokes his ceaseless vitality and unpredictability.

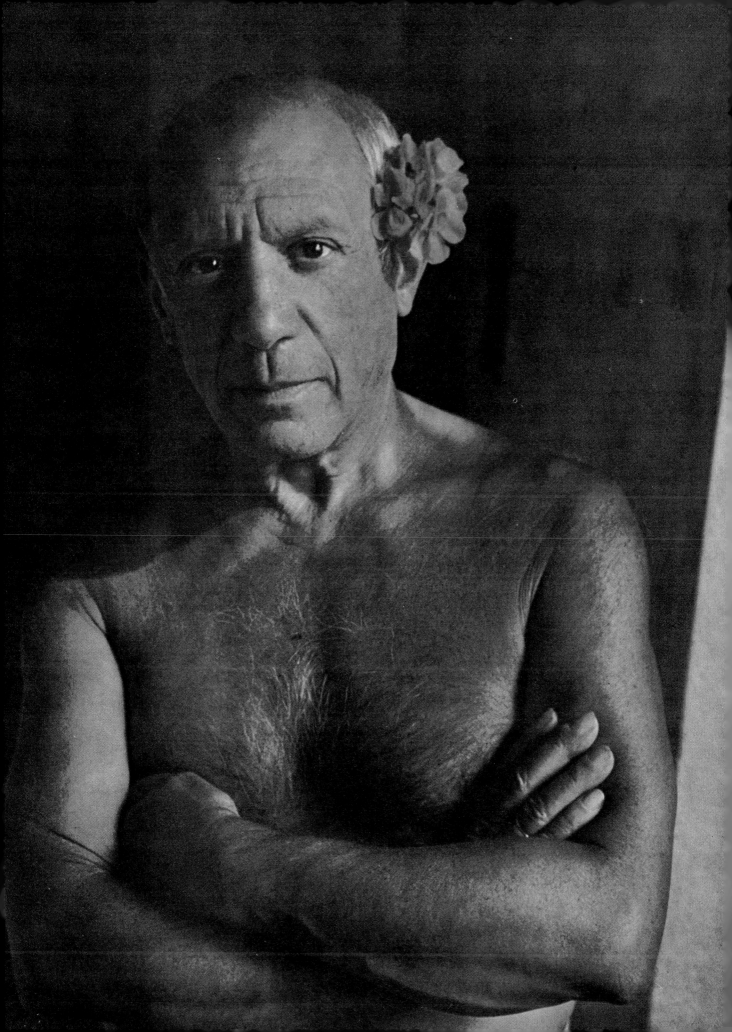

A MONUMENTAL WORK completed by Marc Chagall in 1964 is the ceiling of the Paris Opéra, the old master's brilliant homage to music and ballet in which he shows scenes from a number of favorite stage productions. The huge creation, which Chagall painted in panels at the age of 77, covers a rounded surface 50 feet in diameter.

138

JEAN DUBUFFET, whose canvases are often savage and shocking, leads the *art brut* (raw art) movement in France. He scoffs at the idea of beauty, believes that to be worthwhile a painting must be spontaneous, like the work of an untutored child or a lunatic.

ALBERTO GIACOMETTI, who sculpted stark, skeletal figures that suggest man's isolation, was never satisfied with his work and destroyed his own statues by the dozen. Born in Switzerland, he spent his adult life in Paris and died there, world-celebrated, in 1966.

FRENCH FASHION DESIGNERS,

nourished in the artistic climate of Paris, have long led the world in influence upon women's styles

"COCO" CHANEL, who began designing fashions in 1914, revolutionized women's wear after World War I with the simple sweater and skirt and her famous "little black dress." She felt clothes should free women for their busy new life. Her suits, which barely change over the years, are coveted both in the original and in budget copies.

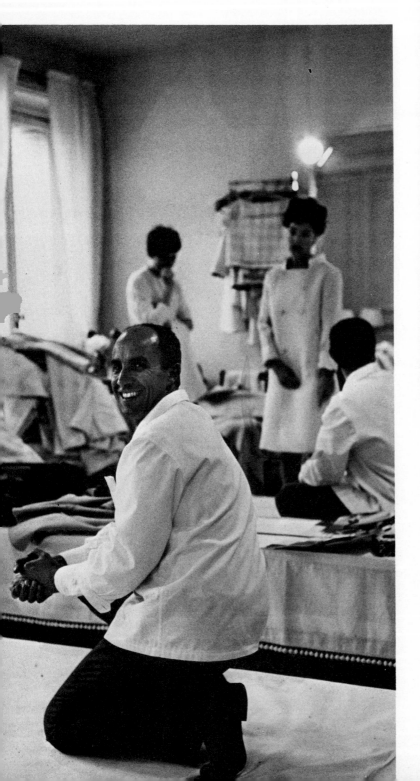

ANDRE COURREGES, shown here in his design workroom, was once an engineer, learned the art of *couture* as an assistant to Balenciaga. He has jumped to the top of the fashion heap in recent years. Believing that "a woman is never more beautiful than when she is naked," he likes to create spare, architectural, "space age" clothes.

YVES SAINT-LAURENT gesticulates with Gallic effusiveness to express an idea about a dress. St.-Laurent rocketed to fame in 1958 when he was chosen at the age of 21 to head the House of Dior. Later forming his own establishment, he has launched some explosive successes—including rectangular designs based on Mondrian paintings.

HELENE LAZAREFF (*right*), the dynamic editor of *Elle*, France's top woman's magazine, chats with a model before a photography session. Mme. Lazareff encourages styles that are gay, young and practical, and has pioneered in promoting the French ready-to-wear trade. Frenchwomen of every walk in life take their fashion cues from *Elle*.

A DOMINANT FIGURE of the French stage for 20 years, actor and director Jean-Louis Barrault has achieved particular success directing plays starring his wife, Madeleine Renaud. Once with the Comédie Française, they now have their own very distinguished company.

A SCENE IN "BECKET," in which Jean Anouilh probes the relationship between England's King Henry II and the Archbishop of Canterbury, is put on stage at a Paris theater. Anouilh's plays, witty and intellectual, have been hits in Paris, London and New York.

day. It enjoys a prestige as great as it had in the 17th Century

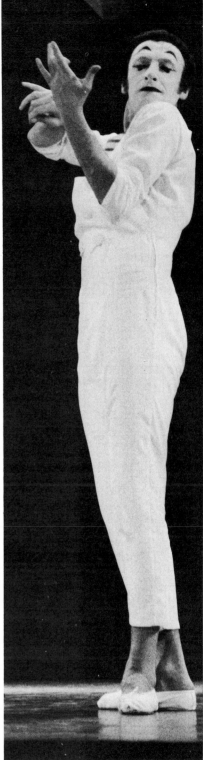

FAMED PANTOMIMIST, Marcel Marceau, who raised the art of voiceless acting to a new level, has been called a "theatrical master of total illusion." His white-face characterization of a clown, Bip (*above*), defeated by life's trials, is one familiar to U.S. television audiences.

143

Tumbling through the air 6,000 feet up, three members of a parachuting club drop arm in arm from a plane in a free fall. At

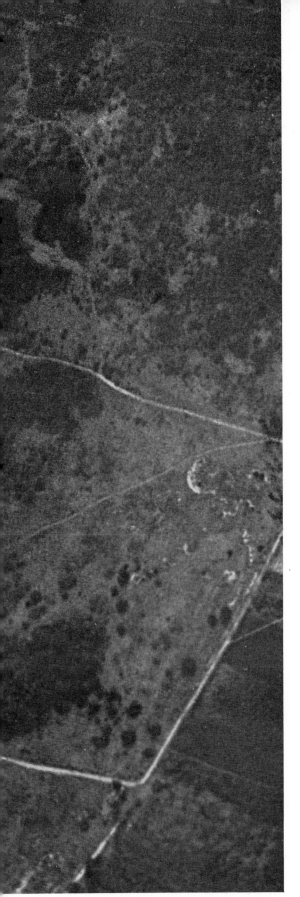

3,000 feet they successfully disengaged and opened their chutes.

9

Strenuous
Uses
of Leisure

THE great 19th Century French diplomat and statesman, Prince Talleyrand, is reported to have remarked that no one who had not lived in France before the Revolution could know the meaning of "the sweetness of life." Speaking as a nobleman of the old order, Talleyrand may have been right. Hunting, for example, was reserved for the nobility (although the exclusive privilege was happily breached by tens of thousands of poachers). But even in France before 1789 foreign visitors like Thomas Jefferson remarked on the amiability, good manners and good sense of the French common people. No one said of them, as the Duc de Sully said of the English in the 17th Century, "They amuse themselves sadly."

Ordinary Frenchmen did indeed take their good times gladly, but their range of pleasure was limited, not only by meager resources but by tradition. They had their saints' feast days and their fairs, and their dances on the village green on a Sunday afternoon. They had, as has been suggested, the illicit pleasure of poaching. But on the whole, leisure was a privilege reserved for their betters.

It is one of the characteristics of the great revolution of modern France that leisure is now much more abundant than before, that it is shared by far more people and that it is used so strenuously. For centuries the overburdened French peasant or worker felt that leisure—because it was scarce—was to be exploited in welcome idleness. The representative French sport was fishing, even in rivers which promised few fish. If there were violent local games like pelota in the Basque region near Spain, the various leisurely forms of lawn bowling were much more widespread. Anyone who was conscripted into the army got all the violent exercise he needed in long marches under an exorbitant weight of weapons and equipment.

A Frenchman born in any century before this would have regarded with astonishment the amount of mere physical endeavor that modern Frenchmen put into *le sport*. As for the now common sight of young Frenchwomen, in hiking shorts, bent double under a pack that would be almost too much for a United States Marine, sunburned and sweating and developing muscles in all the wrong places, this would have struck the Frenchman of old as a subject not so much for wonder as for scandal.

YET the change has come about. Sport, once an eccentric habit of the English, has become almost as much an obsession of the French as it is of the Americans. Of course the privileged classes have always had plenty of leisure, taking it out in games like court tennis (the ancestor of lawn tennis) and hunting. The kings of France were almost pathologically devoted to the chase, and even today in France the pursuit on horseback of deer or wild boar has an aristocratic flavor and ritual which almost conceals the fact that many of the hunters have, in lieu of pedigrees, a modern substitute: money.

Sport in the popular sense was an English importation into France, and it was confined for a long time to the rich. Horse racing in the English style began before the Revolution, but the great tracks in and around Paris—Auteuil, Longchamp and Chantilly—are 19th Century innovations, celebrated in part because they were painted by Toulouse-Lautrec and Degas. By 1865 a French horse, Gladiateur, had won the Derby in England. The Jockey Club had been founded. Race track betting was on the way to being a serious industry. It still is. The very term "pari mutuel" (literally "mutual wager") is French, and although the French do not play the horses as much as the Australians or even the English, they do so much more than the Americans.

Other games were also imported from England, notably rugby, which quickly won its devotees, especially in the South—its speed and violence appealed to the southern temper. Indeed, to many Frenchmen Lourdes is almost as famous for its rugby team as for its shrine.

SOCCER, openly a professional game, is popular all over France, and it excites a great deal of local rivalry. The Algerian rebels brought off an ingenious coup in 1958 when they induced some of the most famous professional soccer players in France, who were Algerian Moslems, to desert their teams and form a "free Algerian" soccer team. This event succeeded in bringing home to many Frenchmen for the first time the degree to which the Arabs of Algeria were "disloyal."

Soccer appeals mainly to the workers, but it does not hold as much fascination for them as does the great indigenous French sport of bicycle racing. There are many local races, but for the average Frenchman the most important of all sporting events is the Tour de France. This grueling physical ordeal lasts for some 20 to 25 days at the height of the summer. The racers, riding some 3,000 miles around the perimeter of France, have to pedal through the South under scorching temperatures and climb mountain passes 7,000 feet high. They are an international lot. In 1965 there were 130 entries from eight countries, all facing the risk of falling down cliffs or being bumped by a competitor.

To be sure, the race is now followed by an ambulance helicopter, and behind the racers is a caravan, miles long, of cars and trucks carrying managers, masseurs, newspaper reporters and traveling exhibits for commercial products like soaps, *apéritifs*, soft drinks and deodorants. Towns pay up to $10,000 to have the racers stop overnight, and all Frenchmen were pleased in 1960 when President de Gaulle came to the roadside near his country house to watch the Tour go past. The leading contestants stopped to shake hands with the president, an unprecedented act of homage.

In the old days the French had a highly skilled form of boxing called *savate* (literally "old, worn-out shoe"), in which the feet were used as well as the fists. But starting in the late 19th Century conventional boxing of the English and American variety became popular. At first a form of exercise among gentlemen, often with paid sparring partners, it became a popular exhibition sport before World War I. For a while mediocre English and American boxers made a good living in Paris, but they were eclipsed after the war by the rise of a number of brilliant French boxers, of whom the most famous was Georges Carpentier. Winning successive championships while rising through all the weight classes and finally becoming light heavyweight champion of the world, Carpentier was rash enough to try for the heavyweight title. He challenged Jack Dempsey—unsuccessfully.

In more recent years the best-known French boxer was the great middleweight Marcel Cerdan, whose death in a plane accident in 1949 was almost certainly lamented more widely among Frenchmen than the passing of the great violinist, Ginette Neveu, who was on the same plane.

COURT tennis has a long history in France, but the more modern game of lawn tennis is far and away more popular. Indeed, women's international competition was for years dominated by Suzanne Lenglen, in her time the most famous of Frenchwomen, more widely known throughout the world than the scientist Marie Curie. Eventually, to the dismay of American tennis fans, Jean Borotra and other skillful French players even managed to win the Davis Cup from the long-dominant Americans and to keep it for six years.

In fact, in every form of sport the French have produced stars, perhaps more stars than winning teams. But the appeal of physical activity has broadened. New games have been imported. Basketball has more than 100,000 players, and the number is growing. Baseball, like cricket, has no appreciable French following, but other sports are flourishing.

IF the development of sport has been revolutionary in modern France, so has the increase in mobility. The bicycle, the motorcycle, the motor scooter and the car have all liberated the French family, the young Frenchman and the young Frenchwoman from the old, confined circle of the village, the small town or even the isolated Paris neighborhood. Once a country of cyclists, France now has very nearly as many cars as bicycles, and the number of cars is rising while the number of bicycles is falling. Many Frenchmen in the cities have always made a practice of keeping in touch with the place their family came from. They often own a rather primitive house in their ancestral village, and they take their holiday among quite remote kinsmen. But more and more the holiday season produces a universal migration, mostly during the month of August, with people moving from every part of France to every other part.

Among the areas most radically affected by this change are the famed resorts. Half a century ago the rich recovered from a winter and spring of overeating and overdrinking by taking to the great spas, of which Vichy was the most famous. There they and tens of thousands of foreigners "took the cure." This mostly involved drinking the mineral waters and undergoing treatment for various real and imaginary ailments, but nearly every spa also had its casino where gambling was legal, its theater and—in the case of the most luxurious ones like Vichy —its race track and golf course. The great spas were, in fact, virtually an extension of Paris.

147

So were the summer seaside resorts, new and old: Trouville and Deauville, Biarritz and Le Touquet. Gambling, love-making, gossip, politics and even mild physical exertion helped a vacationer to pass the time in these resorts. What the French call the Côte d'Azur (the azure coast)—better known to us by its Italian name, the Riviera—owed its importance to the flight of northern Europeans from the horrors of their winter climate. The Promenade des Anglais at Nice recalls the vital role the British played in the creation of the Riviera; Queen Victoria, for example, passed many winters in that neighborhood, far from the character-building weather of her native land. The tiny Mediterranean principality of Monaco in the southeast corner of France gave refuge to great gambling interests, who formed the tactfully named "Society for Sea Bathing," while the great casino provided the background for many real and fictitious dramas.

BUT the modern Riviera is a creation of the period between the two great wars. The 1936 French law requiring paid holidays for all workers bred habits which the new postwar prosperity has greatly extended. Now, far from avoiding the sun of the *Midi*, people flock to it. Sun bathing has become as popular as sea bathing. New resorts like Juan-les-Pins have sprung up, and what was only the preserve of the rich in the winter is now also the resort of people of all classes in the summer.

Since World War II more and more people, most of them young and most only moderately well off, have poured into the *Midi*. The entire coast from the Italian to the Spanish border is now dotted with resorts. Some of these have become famous, smart and expensive almost overnight, like the fishing village of St.-Tropez or "Saint-Trop," the resort of such celebrated figures as Françoise Sagan and Brigitte Bardot. The once placid resort of Cannes is now famous the world over for its film festival, where publicity comes to the aid of art.

But more significant of the social revolution are the inexpensive and socially democratic new beach resorts like Narbonne-Plage on the Mediterranean near Spain. Here trailer camps, cheap hotels, tents and beach cabins all reflect the willingness of Frenchmen to make for the sea and to spend their carefully saved money having a good time. These resorts are not confined to the Mediterranean. They can also be found along the English Channel and the Atlantic coast. One of the most popular of modern French movies, *Mr. Hulot's Holiday*, which made Jacques Tati famous as an actor-writer-director-producer, evokes—albeit satirically—the pleasant surroundings in these resorts, a delight no longer confined to the aristocracy.

SOMETHING like the same democratization of pleasure has marked other forms of entertainment. To be sure, the French theater has always had its "popular" side. But the main tradition of French classical drama has always been aristocratic. The most famous theater in the world, the Comédie-Française, known as the *Maison de Molière*, represents the official interest of the French state in the drama. But the state also subsidizes the Théâtre National Populaire, a "people's theater" whose recent director, Jean Vilar, tried to put the best of theatrical art, French and foreign, within reach of the masses of people who are intimidated by the atmosphere and the prices of the Comédie-Française. Once an ineffectual, moribund organization, the T.N.P. today is booming. Provincial cities subsidize their own theater companies, and everywhere in France the living theater plays a much more important role than it does in Britain or the U.S. France has the richest classical theatrical repertoire of any western nation. But a great deal of the living repertoire is not very classical, and from the point of view of a strict moralist, it is not very edifying either. The most famous Paris theater after the Comédie-Française is the Folies-Bergère, which has been displaying the female form for half a century.

The most potent democratizing force of all in France has been the cinema. In this, as in many other technological advances, the French were pioneers. The Lumière brothers, who developed one of the first movie projectors in 1895, are among the important contributors to the development of motion pictures. France has produced a remarkable number of skilled directors from René Clair to François Truffaut, as well as brilliant performers like the rubber-faced comedian Fernandel and the handsome, versatile character actress Françoise Rosay. Great stage actors and actresses often take parts in motion pictures—more often than the top performers in America—and much of the French cinema has been as highbrow as the repertoire of the Comédie-Française.

But, again like the theater, the cinema has also catered to popular taste. The most famous film star of recent years, Brigitte Bardot, is certainly not a rival of France's two leading serious actresses, Madeleine Renaud and Edwige Feuillère. But, like Françoise Sagan, she is a symbol of revolt against French middle-class life. This is not to deny that most of her French admirers, like most of her American followers, think of her simply as a "sex kitten" rather than as a symbol of any great sociological change.

The seriousness with which the French approach all artistic questions is shown by the immense interest taken in what the critics call "the new wave," a recent series of motion pictures produced by young men often working on a shoestring. Their films frequently have been symbols of revolt against French bourgeois traditions or against war, or pleas for a freer sex life. To the French the cinema is an art as well as a business, and the election of René Clair to the French Academy in 1960 was a belated recognition by an institution founded in the 17th Century of the most novel art form of the 20th.

ANOTHER leveling and unifying force in France has been the radio. During World War II radio probably played a more important role in France than in any other country. It was by radio that the hitherto little-known General de Gaulle in 1940 first appealed to his countrymen from self-imposed exile in Britain, and the French Service of the B.B.C., which both informed the French public on the course of the combat and passed along coded instructions to the underground, was the most effective propaganda service of the war. Every French government since the Liberation used its control of radio for propaganda, and De Gaulle has possibly gone furthest. There are more than 10 million sets in France, and radio programs are often highbrow. The government allots peak listening hours to educational and cultural programs, even though it has reason to believe that listeners might prefer something less edifying.

A SIMILAR willingness to instruct and possibly to bore is shown by the French television network, which is run by the same state organization that controls radio and is paid for by license fees. There are more than six million sets in the country today, and the number increases at the rate of about a million a year. Although TV is still a secondary phenomenon, it is already a democratizing force. Village inhabitants frequently band together to buy a set and form a "teleclub," keeping the set in the village schoolhouse or village hall and paying for it by charging a small entrance fee. This not only brings TV to the farmers but provides what is badly needed in most French villages: a place of common meeting. And thanks to the growth of "Eurovision," a cooperative international TV network, the French are now exposed to programs from England, Germany and Italy as well as to a few filmed American Westerns. This breach of French insularity is going on in all entertainment fields, and it is perhaps significant that one of the most popular male cinema stars in France is an American, Eddie Constantine, who is unknown in his native land.

The older Frenchman, slowly sipping a drink and playing dominoes in a café, can hardly help raising an eyebrow when he sees the younger generation gazing at the TV screen in a bar or shooting off on bicycles, motor scooters or cars. He is the witness, and not always the pleased witness, of a revolution in French folkways. Dominoes and fishing are not energetic enough for the leisure of the "new wave" of young French men and women.

A Gallic Enthusiasm for Sport

While the Frenchman of legend may despise all outdoor physical activity, Gallic sportsmen today have earned a large reputation for rugged types of exertion. Men of France have climbed the frostiest Himalayas and dropped to record depths underground; one of them pioneered the sport of skin diving. The Tour de France is the world's most grueling event for cyclists, and for sports-car drivers the race at Le Mans is perhaps the world's most demanding. Even the French government enhances the national vigor with a program for promoting physical fitness.

SCALING THE HEIGHTS, mountain climber Gaston Rebuffat waves from the pinnacle of the ice-covered 10,227-foot Aiguille de Roc (needle of rock) in the French Alps.

PEDALING UP A HILL (*opposite*), bicyclists of the Tour de France speed through Lessines in Belgium on an early leg of the annual race. Injuries to contestants are frequent.

PROBING THE DEPTHS, spelunkers test for leaks in their waterproof suits by dipping their feet in a stalagmite-surrounded lake 1,621 feet underground near Grenoble.

*OUTDOOR RELAXATION is a favorite occupation of the French,
who are characterized by a genius for capturing the 'sweetness of life'*

HOLIDAYMAKERS, well protected against the sea breezes, take the air at Trouville on the Normandy coast. The entire population of France appears to head outdoors in August. Paris goes suddenly empty, with so many shopkeepers on vacation for the month that tourists often have difficulty finding a laundry or grocery store open.

OLD FRIENDS get together in Provence for an afternoon of *boules*. The game, something like a cross between bowling and billiards, is traditionally the sport of middle-aged men of the *Midi*, but is played by many others as well.

A FRENCH FAMILY enjoys a roadside luncheon, complete with wine, in a scene that can be found repeated all over the country in the summertime. Even the smallest French car has room for a picnic table and chairs on top.

IN THE DEEP, a French swimmer sights a shark and its pilot fish. His aqualung, developed by the French diver Jacques Cousteau, provoked the world skin-diving boom.

IN THE SUN, a bikini-clad girl basks on a bathing barge on the Seine. Floating swimming pools, these barges are anchored conveniently at the river embankment in Paris.

SPORTS CAR RACING *culminates in the grueling*
24-hour race at Le Mans, an event which
annually draws up to a quarter of a million spectators

ACTION ON THE COURSE begins as the drivers sprint across the road (*left*) to jump into their cars and start the long race.

A BEGOGGLED DRIVER careens past in a Jaguar. Roaring by night and day, the cars often make speeds as high as 165 mph.

A **STEEPLECHASE** is run off at Auteuil, a track on the edge of the Bois de Boulogne in Paris. "Auteuil represents heaven on earth: champagne, pretty women, good horses," in the words of one reverent French sportsman.

CANADA

DENMARK

FRANCE

GREECE

ICELAND

ITALY

LUXEMBOURG

NETHERLANDS

NORWAY

PORTUGAL

TURKEY

UNITED KINGDOM

UNITED STATES

SOLEMN MOMENT in Paris
occurs for France in 1954 as
Germany, an old enemy, is
brought into NATO. Here
Belgium's Paul Henri Spaak
signs. Rear: the Eiffel Tower.

10

A Changing
Role Before
the World

"WHEN Paris sneezes, Europe catches cold."
This famous jest, more than a century old, recalls a time when France was still the dominant power in Europe, a threat to the independence of her neighbors and a promise of aid to the discontented far and near. That France went down to defeat in 1871 and has not reappeared. The 1918 victory was bought at too great a cost and was too visibly the triumph of an alliance to breed new delusions of grandeur.

Although France was formally victorious in World War II, she was nearly as much a defeated nation as Germany or Italy. Indeed, many people inside and outside France in 1945 doubted if she could maintain her own independence, much less lead others. France, they felt, had better concentrate on cultivating her own garden and leave the great issues to the really great powers, the United States and Russia. Some faith might be put in the United Nations; more might be put in the growth of the French Union, which had replaced the French empire. But France had to learn to live within her means, and these means were very limited.

Subsequent developments served to underline this attitude. One event was the rapid economic recovery which followed the introduction of U.S. Marshall Plan aid. Another was the coming of the cold war, which made France, for geographical as well as political reasons, a cornerstone of the defense system set up to resist Russian pressure. Both of these events had been made possible to a large extent by the power of the United States. Neither invalidated the view that the French power of independent action was limited.

The power of France today is far greater than seemed probable as late as 1948, for France is very much richer than was anticipated. Yet that wealth was drained away for more than 10 years by two disastrous colonial wars, one in Indochina and then one in Algeria. France could not have an effective military policy of any kind so long as these two wars went on. The Algerian war necessitated stationing the greater part of the French army in Algeria and this made it impossible for France to meet her commitments to the North Atlantic Treaty Organization (NATO), and the kind of army needed in Algeria was useless for modern warfare in Europe.

ONE consequence of the diversion of French military resources was that the United States rightly thought that Britain and West Germany were more valuable as military allies than France. And the abortive Anglo-French attack on Egypt in 1956 revealed how limited was the power of independent action left either to France or to Britain.

The return of General de Gaulle to power in 1958 caused an apprehension among France's allies that would prove to be in part justified. General de Gaulle had not, during his exile from power, shown any enthusiasm for "Europe" or for the integration of French forces in the NATO alliance. Would his attitude change?

The worst of the political fears were not realized. The De Gaulle government accepted and indeed developed the French commitment in the Common Market. But De Gaulle is above all a nationalist, and his attitude toward the Common Market—as toward NATO and toward European integration as a whole—has been ambivalent. The general could never equably view the Common Market as a supreme body whose authority would take precedence over France. In 1965, when the question came to a head in agricultural negotiations, he temporarily boycotted meetings of "the Six," even though it meant hardship for French farmers.

HIS allies had been right in fearing that De Gaulle would be an awkward partner in NATO. Despite the ending of the Algerian war and the return to France of the greater part of the French army in Algeria, the general did not put these troops at the disposal of NATO. He refused to take part in various American schemes for strengthening the land-sea-air forces of NATO and insisted on continuing his attempts to create an independent French atomic bombing force.

By American (or Russian) standards, the French bomb was not very formidable, nor the means of delivery very efficacious. Many Frenchmen felt that the "force de frappe" (as it was called) was a pointless luxury that France could not afford. They felt that the immense expenditure of billions of dollars could be better devoted to more schools, houses or hospitals or even to a better-equipped army.

But it was difficult to think of any argument against France's having an atomic weapon that did not apply equally to Britain. Nationalist groups in French society were gratified by De Gaulle's success in forcing NATO to remove its nuclear bombing squadrons from France. The French government was in effect refusing to permit the stockpiling in France of atomic weapons in whose control it did not have, in De Gaulle's opinion, an adequate share.

Another source of friction was De Gaulle's insistence on the independence of the national forces contributed to NATO. He claimed for France a degree of military autonomy which suggested that the great military pioneer of the 1930s had settled down to a form of military conservatism which could be very dangerous.

From the point of view of the French people, President de Gaulle's greatest achievement was the ending of the Algerian war. This triumph had its paradoxical aspects, since it was in order to save "French Algeria" that military and civilian conspirators in Algiers began the movement that brought De Gaulle back to power. Whatever General de Gaulle thought of the Algerian problem before he came to power, he finally decided that terms must be made with the Algerian nationalists. It soon became apparent to the military leaders in Algeria that General de Gaulle was not going to carry out their policy. It was equally apparent to certain civilian ministers that the General was going to prove the very opposite of an ally in keeping Algeria French.

IT could have been argued that the soldiers and politicians had some right on their side when they said that De Gaulle deceived them. A sense of desperation struck both the soldiers and the "colons," the French landowners in Algeria, as the General's policy became evident. For the "colons," Algerian independence meant ruin and exile, and their fears were justified. But it became evident to General de Gaulle that there was no substitute for Algerian nationalism and he finally accepted the complete independence of Algeria.

This sense of betrayal produced in Algeria a series of mutinies and conspiracies. It also deeply exacerbated the race war in Algeria as the so-called "Secret Army" or OAS (Organisation de l'Armée Secrète) plunged into an orgy of indiscriminate crime directed against the indigenous population. All the conspiracies and all the mutinies failed. And Algeria was given its independence by the Evian Accords of 1962.

But the poison of the war was not totally eliminated by the acceptance of Algerian independence. Hundreds of thousands of Europeans fled to France, a country of which they knew little, and to a new industrial society for which they were ill-equipped. The government spent vast sums of money on rehabilitation but the newcomers preferred to settle in the south of France, where the climate suited them better, and avoided settling in those regions which were underpopulated or which needed unskilled labor. In this atmosphere, the habit of conspiracy was transferred from Algeria to France.

True, there was much less crime among the "colons" than had been anticipated. But the "Secret Army" was a source of mischief all the same. The assassination of General de Gaulle was repeatedly attempted and some of the attempts very nearly succeeded. There were outbursts of gangster warfare in Marseilles and in Paris. The initials of the OAS were used as a cover for attempted blackmail of such national figures as Brigitte Bardot and Françoise Sagan. Some bold murders were committed in the very heart of Paris, and France was shocked by the scandal of the former Resistance leader, Georges Bidault, accepting the nominal command of the conspiracy.

And if the Algerian leaders discovered that they needed French help more than France needed Algerian resources, nevertheless they pushed ahead with the uprooting of the French economic and social structure built up over 130 years. Furthermore, the newly independent Algeria found it profitable to be a partner of France, but a partner on equal terms.

MANY Frenchmen today, viewing the last half century in perspective, think that France's real role in the present world is what the French call *rayonnement* (spreading cultural and intellectual light). They have immense confidence in the attractiveness of French culture, and British observers in Africa have noted, rather ruefully, that the ex-French colonies, even the ex-colony of Guinea which for a time preferred association with Communists, have a much more "French" elite than have the British ex-colonies a "British" counterpart, and that they produce, on the whole, more sagacious leaders.

The Frenchmen of this school hope that—despite the horrible memories of the Algerian war—Algeria, as Tunisia and Morocco have done, will forgive the old imperial power and remain a partner of France and not simply another "Arab" country.

The same school of thought in France feels that France lost an unusually good chance of leadership in Europe in the years after the end of World War II. Britain abdicated her position of natural leadership and some of the most fruitful ideas about Europe came from great Frenchmen like Robert Schuman and Jean Monnet. It is possible that most of the small nations of Europe would have followed a French lead if the government of the Fourth Republic had been capable of giving an effective lead. It was not.

De Gaulle brought a renewal of leadership—but in what direction? Whereas many active proponents of European unity looked forward to attaining their goal by building up the supranational economic bodies already in existence, De Gaulle was willing to downgrade these bodies in favor of closer governmental collaboration at the top. At first he supported the idea of a European parliament made up of the members of the Common Market, with delegates from the national parliament of each state. But by 1966 he was firm in his view that the union of the six countries should be purely economic, and that to sacrifice political sovereignty to a central authority would be, for France at least, a mistake.

DE GAULLE showed in other ways that he was extremely jealous of the sovereignty of France. He proposed more than once that inside NATO there should be a directorate of three powers, the United States, Britain and France —a proposal disliked by all of France's European allies. His European schemes called for a union of governments more than a union of peoples, and of governments controlling with jealous independence their own military resources.

This concept seems narrow to those people who hope to see France recover by peaceful means, by cultural rather than material superiority, the leadership she lost in the last century and a half. Certain changes to the disadvantage of France cannot be undone. The population balance of Europe and the world has shifted against her. Though French is still a world language, it is no longer *the* world language.

Nevertheless it is an astonishing tribute to the vitality of France's culture that so much of the world's business, above all its intellectual business, is still done in French. Paris has not lost her old attractions for the pleasure-seekers and the seekers after wisdom. To Paris flock thousands of students from all over the world, as they have throughout the centuries.

THERE is another aspect to the continuing prestige of French culture. The French are much less intellectually isolationist than they were. The self-confidence that has come with economic expansion has brought with it a more objective assessment of the true position of France and an acceptance of the fact that she will never again impose her will by arms or cast the last word in the decisions of the really great powers.

But a solvent, expanding France that is part of a solvent and expanding Europe may play a role in the future at least as impressive as was France's role in the past. It will be a different one, however. A popular 19th Century painting shows French soldiers dreaming of the triumphant charge of Napoleon's troops. The title of the picture is *The Dream*. That dream haunts fewer and fewer French minds today. A more hopeful dream, one that haunts more and more French minds, is of competition and collaboration in the arts and sciences, of help given on terms of equality to the nations struggling to birth, of leadership offered to the world in the organization of a varied and human culture.

Athens, it is said, was "the eye of Greece." The French hope with reason that France will be an eye, if not *the* eye, of a new and more peaceful world. The final decision about peace and war does not lie in French hands. But if the decision is for peace, the new French dream and achievement may be as glorious as in the days of French political and military dominance.

French rocket technicians prepare to launch an earth satellite. Next page: Visitors swarm through the ornate galleries of the Louvre.

ON THE THRESHOLD *of a new era, France's historic dream of glory...*

... is coupled with a vision of France 'spreading the light' culturally to ot

tions, giving new meaning to the old cry, 'Liberty, equality, fraternity'

Appendix

HISTORICAL DATES

B.C.

600   Massilia (Marseilles) is founded by the Greeks

500   Celts invade from across the Rhine and establish themselves in the area that the Romans call Gaul

390   Celts (whom the Romans call Gauls) sack Rome

121   Romans occupy the Mediterranean shores of Gaul

58-51   Julius Caesar conquers Gaul

52   Romans capture Lutetia, the fortified town of the Gallic tribe of Parisii; the town is later renamed Paris

A.D.

257   Franks and Alamans invade Gaul from across the Rhine

406   New invasions of Germanic tribes (the Vandals, Alamans and Burgundians) usher in the so-called Dark Ages

451   Huns under Attila are turned back at Châlons by a combined Gallo-Roman and Visigothic army

496   Baptism of Clovis, the first real "King of France" and founder of the Merovingian Dynasty

714-741   Rule of Charles Martel, "mayor of the palace"

732   Charles Martel defeats the Arabs near Tours, ending a Moslem invasion of France

751   Pepin the Short, mayor of the palace, becomes king and establishes the Carolingian Dynasty (so called after Charlemagne, its most illustrious member)

768-814   Reign of Charlemagne

800   Charlemagne is crowned emperor by the Pope

911   Raiding Normans are granted the northwestern region of France, which later becomes the duchy of Normandy

987   Hugh Capet, Count of Paris, is elected king and establishes the Capetian Dynasty

987-1328   Capetians extend the power of the monarchy

1226-1270   Reign of St. Louis (Louis IX), the greatest medieval French king

1328-1589   Reign of the Valois branch of the Capetian Dynasty

1337-1453   Hundred Years' War between France and England

1415   Battle of Agincourt; English longbowmen defeat a superior number of French knights

1429   Joan of Arc causes Charles VII to be crowned at Reims

1560-1598   Wars of the Reformation in France

1572   Massacre of the Huguenots on St. Bartholomew's Eve

1589-1610   Reign of Henry IV; the start of the Bourbon Dynasty

1598   Henry IV issues the Edict of Nantes, granting toleration to the Protestants

1643-1715   Reign of Louis XIV, the "Sun King"; the high point of the absolute monarchy

1685   Louis XIV revokes the Edict of Nantes

1704   French are defeated at the Battle of Blenheim by the English (under the Duke of Marlborough) and the Austrians (under Prince Eugene)

1715-1774   Reign of Louis XV; the power of the monarchy declines

1756-1763   Seven Years' War; France loses India and Canada to England, Louisiana to Spain

1774-1792   Reign of Louis XVI, the last absolute monarch

1789   Meeting of the Estates-General; the French Revolution begins

1792   Louis XVI is dethroned

1792-1799   The First Republic

1792   Wars of the French Revolution begin with France fighting Austria and Prussia

1793   War expands as major European powers unite against France

1799-1804   The Consulate under Napoleon

1804-1814   The First Empire under Napoleon

1812   Napoleon's armies retreat from Moscow

1814   Napoleon is exiled to Elba; the Bourbons are restored under Louis XVIII

1814-1824   Reign of Louis XVIII

1815   Napoleon returns, is defeated at the Battle of Waterloo, and is exiled to St. Helena

1824-1830   Reign of Charles X

1830   The July Revolution (caused by discontent with Charles X's reactionary policies) brings to power Louis Philippe I (the Orleans branch of the Bourbon Dynasty)

1848   The Revolution of 1848 establishes the Second Republic; Louis Napoleon (nephew of Napoleon Bonaparte) is elected president

1852   Louis Napoleon stages a *coup d'état;* the empire is restored by popular vote; Louis Napoleon becomes Emperor Napoleon III

1852-1870   The Second Empire under Napoleon III

1870   France is invaded by Prussia; the Second Empire falls and the Third Republic is proclaimed

1871   France is defeated by Prussia and loses Alsace and Lorraine; the insurrection of the Paris Commune

1870-1940   The Third Republic

1894-1899   The Dreyfus affair (Capt. Alfred Dreyfus is wrongly accused of treason) shakes the Third Republic, but ultimately results in the discrediting of rightists and militarists; Socialists and Radicals gain influence

1914-1918   World War I; the Allies defeat Germany

1919   France recovers Alsace-Lorraine under the Versailles treaty

1936-1937   The Popular Front, a Socialist government under Léon Blum

1939   World War II begins

1940   France falls under the German blitzkrieg; the end of the Third Republic; General Charles de Gaulle heads Free French forces in London

1940-1944   The Vichy regime under Pétain and Laval rules Occupied France

1944   Allied forces liberate France

1944-1946   Provisional government under De Gaulle

1946-1958   The Fourth Republic

1954   Fall of Dienbienphu leads to the loss of Indochina

1958   Algerian crisis brings the Fourth Republic to an end; General de Gaulle returns to power; the Fifth Republic is established

1962   Eight-year Algerian war ends with Algerian independence

1965   Re-election of General de Gaulle as President of the Republic

CHAPTER 1: FRANCE TODAY

Borel, Pierre, *Côte d'Azur (The French Riviera)*. Oxford University Press, 1957.

Brion, Marcel, *Provence*. Oxford University Press, 1957.

Clark, Sydney, *All the Best in France*. Dodd, Mead & Company, 1958.

Clark, Sydney, *Today in Cathedral France* (revised edition). Robert M. McBride & Company, 1948.

Dutton, Ralph, *Normandy and Brittany*. B. T. Batsford Ltd., London, 1953.

Hoffman, Stanley, and others, *In Search of France*. Harvard University Press, 1963.

Ogrizek, Doré, editor, *France; A Portrait in Color*. McGraw-Hill Book Company, Inc., 1959.

Spengler, Joseph, *France Faces Depopulation*. Duke University Press, 1938.

Tannenbaum, Edward R., *The New France*. University of Chicago Press, 1961.

Wylie, Laurence, *Village in the Vaucluse*. Harvard University Press, 1957.

CHAPTER 2: HISTORY (GENERAL)

Davis, William Stearns, *A History of France; From the Earliest Times to the Treaty of Versailles*. Houghton Mifflin Company, 1919.

Guérard, Albert, *France; A Modern History*. University of Michigan Press, 1959.

Guignebert, Charles, *A Short History of the French People* (2 vols.). The Macmillan Company, 1930.

Maurois, André, *A History of France*. Farrar, Straus and Cudahy, 1956.

Romier, Lucien, and A. L. Rowse, *A History of France*. St. Martin's Press, 1953.

Seignobos, Charles, *The Evolution of the French People*. Alfred A. Knopf, 1932.

CHAPTER 2: HISTORY (BY PERIODS)

Funck-Brentano, Fr., *The Earliest Times*. G. P. Putnam's Sons, 1927.

Evans, Joan, *Life in Medieval France*. Phaidon Publishers Inc., 1957.

Batiffol, Louis, *The Century of the Renaissance*. G. P. Putnam's Sons, 1935.

Lewis, W. H., *The Splendid Century*. William Sloane Associates, 1954.

Boulenger, Jacques, *The Seventeenth Century*. G. P. Putnam's Sons, 1933.

Taine, Hippolyte Adolphe, *The Ancient Régime*. Henry Holt and Company, 1876.

Salvemini, Gaetano, *The French Revolution, 1788-1792*. Henry Holt and Company, 1954.

Bainville, Jacques, *Napoleon*. Little, Brown and Company, 1933.

Brogan, D. W., *The French Nation; From Napoleon to Pétain*. Harper & Brothers, 1957.

Lucas-Dubreton, J., *The Restoration and the July Monarchy*. G. P. Putnam's Sons, 1929.

Thompson, J. M., *Louis Napoleon and the Second Empire*. The Noonday Press, 1955.

Brogan, D. W., *France Under the Republic; The Development of Modern France, 1870-1939*. Harper & Brothers, 1940.

Thomson, David, *Democracy in France; The Third Republic*. Oxford University Press, 1946.

Werth, Alexander, *The Twilight of France, 1933-1940*. Harper & Brothers, 1942.

Aron, Robert, *The Vichy Regime, 1940-1944*. The Macmillan Company, 1958.

De Gaulle, Charles, *The War Memoirs of Charles de Gaulle: The Call to Honour, 1940-1942*, The Viking Press, 1955; *Unity, 1942-1944*, Simon and Schuster, 1959; *Salvation, 1944-1946*, Simon and Schuster, 1960.

CHAPTER 3: GOVERNMENT AND POLITICS

Aron, Raymond, *France Steadfast and Changing*. Harvard University Press, 1960.

Chapman, Brian, *Introduction to French Local Government*. George Allen & Unwin Ltd., London, 1953.

Chapman, Brian, *The Prefects and Provincial France*. George Allen & Unwin Ltd., London, 1955.

Clark, Stanley, *The Man Who Is France; The Story of General Charles de Gaulle*. Dodd, Mead & Company, 1960.

Duverger, Maurice, *The French Political System*. University of Chicago Press, 1958.

Earle, Edward Mead, editor, *Modern France; Problems of the Third and Fourth Republics*. Princeton University Press, 1951.

Furniss, Edgar S. Jr., *France, Troubled Ally; De Gaulle's Heritage and Prospects*. Harper & Brothers, 1960.

Leites, Nathan, *On the Game of Politics in France*. Stanford University Press, 1959.

Luethy, Herbert, *France Against Herself; A Perceptive Study of France's Past, Her Politics, and Her Unending Crises*. Frederick A. Praeger, 1955.

Pickles, Dorothy, *The Fifth French Republic*. Frederick A. Praeger, 1960.

Pickles, Dorothy, *French Politics; The First Years of the Fourth Republic*. Royal Institute of International Affairs, 1953.

Werth, Alexander, *France, 1940-1955*. Henry Holt and Company, 1956.

Werth, Alexander, *The Strange History of Pierre Mendès-France and the Great Conflict over French North Africa*. Barrie Books Ltd., London, 1957.

Williams, Philip M., *Politics in Post-War France; Parties and the Constitution in the Fourth Republic* (second edition). Longmans, Green and Co., 1958.

Williams, Philip M., and Martin Harrison, *De Gaulle's Republic*. Longmans, Green and Co., 1960.

CHAPTERS 4, 5: TRADE, INDUSTRY AND AGRICULTURE

Alpert, Paul, *Twentieth Century Economic History of Europe*. Henry Schuman, 1951.

Baum, Warren C., *The French Economy and the State*. Princeton University Press, 1958.

Clough, Shepard Bancroft, *France; A History of National Economics, 1789-1939*. Charles Scribner's Sons, 1939.

Committee for Economic Development, *The European Common Market & Its Meaning to the United States*. McGraw-Hill Book Company, Inc., 1959.

Committee on Foreign Affairs, U.S. Congress, *A Study of European Economic Regionalism—A New Era in Free World Economic Politics*. U.S. Government Printing Office, 1960.

Day, Clive, *Economic Development in Europe*. The Macmillan Company, 1942.

Diebold, William Jr., *The Schuman Plan; A Study in Economic Cooperation, 1950-59*. Frederick A. Praeger, 1959.

France From Reconstruction to Expansion, 1948-58. French Embassy Press and Information Service, 1958.

Lichine, Alexis, *Wines of France*. Alfred A. Knopf, 1955.

Ogburn, William F., and William Jaffé, *The Economic Development of Post-War France; A Survey of Production*. Columbia University Press, 1929.

Ormsby, H., *France; A Regional and Economic Geography* (second revised edition). E. P. Dutton & Co., Inc., 1950.

CHAPTER 7: EDUCATION AND RELIGION

The Catholic Encyclopedia, Vol. 6. The Encyclopedia Press Inc., 1909.

Cramer, John Francis, and George Stephenson Browne, *Contemporary Education; A Comparative Study of National Systems*. Harcourt, Brace and Company, 1956.

Galton, Arthur, *Church and State in France, 1300-1907*. Edward Arnold, London, 1907.

Keller, Adolf, and George Stewart, *Protestant Europe: Its Crisis and Outlook*. George H. Boran Company, 1927.

Phillips, C. S., *The Church in France, 1789-1848: A Study in Revival*. A. R. Mowbray & Co., Ltd., London, 1929.

Phillips, C. S., *The Church in France, 1848-1907*. The Macmillan Company, 1936.

Reisner, Edward H., *Nationalism and Education Since 1789*. The Macmillan Company, 1923.

The Universal Jewish Encyclopedia, Vol. 4, 1941.

CHAPTERS 6, 8, 9: PHILOSOPHY, ARTS AND LETTERS

Blackham, H. J., *Six Existentialist Thinkers*. Harper & Brothers, 1959.

Brée, Germaine, and Margaret Guiton, *An Age of Fiction; The French Novel from Gide to Camus*. Rutgers University Press, 1957.

Brereton, Geoffrey, *A Short History of French Literature*. Penguin Books, 1954.

Fowlie, Wallace, *Dionysus in Paris; A Guide to Contemporary French Theater*. Meridian Books, Inc., 1960.

Fowlie, Wallace, *A Guide to Contemporary French Literature from Valéry to Sartre*. Meridian Books, Inc., 1957.

Harvey, Sir Paul, and J. E. Heseltine, *The Oxford Companion to French Literature*. Oxford University Press, 1959.

Havens, George R., *The Age of Ideas; From Reaction to Revolution in Eighteenth-Century France*. Henry Holt and Company, 1955.

Lang, Paul Henry, *Music in Western Civilization*. W. W. Norton & Company, Inc., 1941.

Park, Julian, editor, *The Culture of France in Our Time*. Cornell University Press, 1954.

Picken, Mary Brooks, and Dora Loues Miller, *Dressmakers of France; The Who, How and Why of the French Couture*. Harper & Brothers, 1956.

Rolland, Romain, André Maurois and Edouard Herriot, *French Thought in the Eighteenth Century; Rousseau, Voltaire and Diderot*. David McKay Company, Inc., 1953.

Wahl, Jean, *A Short History of Existentialism*. Philosophical Library, 1949.

Wilenski, R. H., *French Painting* (revised edition). Charles T. Branford Company, 1949.

Wilenski, R. H., *Modern French Painters* (Vol. I, 1863-1903; Vol. II, 1904-1938). Vintage Books, 1960.

CHAPTER 10: FRANCE AND THE WORLD
Aron, Raymond, and August Heckscher.

Diversity of Worlds; France and the United States Look at Their Common Problems. Reynal & Company, 1957.

Cady, John F., *The Roots of French Imperialism in Eastern Asia*. Cornell University Press, 1954.

Clark, Michael K., *Algeria in Turmoil*. Frederick A. Praeger, 1959.

Deschamps, Hubert, *The French Union*. Editions Berger-Levrault, Paris, 1956.

Hahn, Lorna, *North Africa; Nationalism to Nationhood*. Public Affairs Press, 1960.

Hammer, Ellen J., *The Struggle for Indochina*. Stanford University Press, 1954.

McKay, Donald C., *The United States and France*. Harvard University Press, 1951.

Priestly, Herbert Ingram, *France Overseas Through the Old Régime; A Study of European Expansion*. D. Appleton-Century Company, 1939.

Stern, Jacques, *The French Colonies Past and Future*. Didier, 1944.

Thompson, Virginia, and Richard Adloff, *French West Africa*. Stanford University Press, 1958.

FAMOUS FRENCH CULTURAL FIGURES AND THEIR PRINCIPAL WORKS

MUSIC

Machaut, Guillaume de	c.1300-1372	Ballads, motets and masses. *Messe Notre Dame* (first known setting of mass in four parts)
Le Jeune, Claude	1528-1600	Songs, masses, motets, madrigals
Lully, Jean Baptiste	1632-1687	Development of the form of French opera
Couperin (*le Grand*), François	1668-1733	Harpsichord and instrumental music, secular songs, church music
Rameau, Jean Philippe	1683-1764	Development of harmonic theory. Operas: *Hippolyte and Aricie, Castor and Pollux*
Berlioz, Hector	1803-1869	*Fantastic Symphony, Harold in Italy, Romeo and Juliet*
Lalo, Edouard	1823-1892	*Spanish Symphony, The King of Ys, Namouna*
Saint-Saëns, Camille	1835-1921	*Samson and Delilah, Third Symphony*
Bizet, Georges	1838-1875	*Carmen*
Chabrier, Emmanuel	1841-1894	*España, The King in Spite of Himself*
Fauré, Gabriel	1845-1924	*Requiem Mass, La Bonne Chanson* (song cycle), *Masques et Bergamasques* (suite), other songs and piano music
Debussy, Claude	1862-1918	*Pelléas and Mélisande, Prelude to the Afternoon of a Faun, La Mer*
Ravel, Maurice	1875-1937	*Gaspard de la Nuit* (for piano), *Daphnis and Chloë* (ballet), *L'Enfant et les Sortilèges* (opera)
Milhaud, Darius	1892-	*Christopher Columbus* (opera), ballets, symphonies, concertos, chamber music
Honegger, Arthur	1892-1955	*King David* (oratorio), *Jeanne d'Arc au Bûcher*, symphonies, operas, ballets, chamber music, piano music, songs
Poulenc, Francis	1899-	Ballets, orchestral works, chamber music, piano music, songs

LITERATURE

Villon, François	1431- ?	*The Legacies, or Small Testament; The Testament*
Rabelais, François	1497?-c.1553	*Gargantua, Pantagruel*
Montaigne, Michel de	1533-1592	*Essays*
Descartes, René	1596-1650	*Discourse on Method, Treatise on the Passions of the Soul, Meditations, Principles of Philosophy*
Corneille, Pierre	1606-1684	Master of classical tragedy: *Le Cid, Horace, Cinna*
La Fontaine, Jean de	1621-1695	*Fables, Contes et Nouvelles* (Tales)
Molière (Jean-Baptiste Poquelin)	1622-1673	Comedies: *L'Avare* (The Miser), *Le Bourgeois Gentilhomme* (The Would-Be Gentleman), *Le Malade Imaginaire* (The Hypochondriac), *The Misanthrope, Amphytrion, Tartuffe*
Pascal, Blaise	1623-1662	*Pensées, Provincial Letters*
Racine, Jean	1639-1699	Tragedies: *Andromaque, Phèdre, Athalie, Britannicus*
Montesquieu, Charles de Secondat, Baron de	1689-1755	*Persian Letters, The Spirit of the Laws*
Voltaire (François-Marie Arouet)	1694-1778	*Candide* (novel), *Letters Concerning the English Nation, Zaïre* (tragedy)
Rousseau, Jean-Jacques	1712-1778	*Emile* (novel), *The Social Contract, Confessions*
Diderot, Denis	1713-1784	*Rameau's Nephew, Jacques the Fatalist*. Founder and editor of the *Encyclopédie*
Stendhal (Henri Beyle)	1783-1842	*The Red and the Black, The Charterhouse of Parma*

Balzac, Honoré de	1799-1850	Novels: *Eugénie Grandet, Le Père Goriot, Les Illusions Perdues, La Cousine Bette*
Hugo, Victor	1802-1885	Novels: *Notre-Dame de Paris, Les Misérables, The Toilers of the Sea.* Poems: *Les Contemplations*
Flaubert, Gustave	1821-1880	Novels: *Madame Bovary, Salammbô*
Baudelaire, Charles	1821-1867	Collection of poems: *Les Fleurs du Mal (Flowers of Evil)*
Zola, Emile	1840-1902	Novels: *L'Assommoir (The Dram-Shop), Germinal, L'Argent (Money), Nana*
Verlaine, Paul	1844-1896	Collections of poems: *Sagesse, Romances sans Paroles, Jadis et Naguère*
Maupassant, Guy de	1850-1893	Short stories: *Boule-de-Suif (Tallow Ball), La Ficelle (The Piece of String).* Novels: *Pierre et Jean, Bel-Ami*
Rimbaud, Arthur	1854-1891	*Le Bateau Ivre* (poem), *Une Saison en Enfer (A Season in Hell*—memoirs)
Claudel, Paul	1868-1955	Plays: *The Satin Slipper, Tidings Brought to Mary*
Gide, André	1869-1951	Novels: *Fruits of the Earth, The Immoralist, Pastoral Symphony, The Counterfeiters, Strait Is the Gate*
Valéry, Paul	1871-1945	Poems: *La Jeune Parque, Le Cimetière Marin.* Prose: *An Evening with Mr. Teste*
Proust, Marcel	1871-1922	Novel cycle: *Remembrance of Things Past*
Colette (Sidonie-Gabrielle)	1873-1954	Novels: *Chéri, Le Blé en Herbe, La Chatte*
Giraudoux, Jean	1882-1944	Plays: *Tiger at the Gates, Electra, The Madwoman of Chaillot, Ondine*
Mauriac, François	1885-	Novels: *Thérèse Desqueyroux, Viper's Tangle, The Lamb*
Perse, Saint-John (Alexis Léger)	1887-	Nobel prize-winning poetry: *Anabase, Eloges, Amers*
Cocteau, Jean	1892-1963	Plays: *La Machine Infernale, Les Parents Terribles.* Films: *Beauty and the Beast, Blood of a Poet*
Montherlant, Henry de	1896-	Plays: *La Reine Morte, Port-Royal*
Malraux, André	1901-	*Man's Fate, Man's Hope* (novels), *The Psychology of Art*
Sartre, Jean-Paul	1905-	*Being and Nothingness, Existentialism.* Novels: *Nausea, The Age of Reason.* Plays: *The Flies, No Exit, The Respectful Prostitute, Red Hands*
Anouilh, Jean	1910-	Plays: *Antigone, Legend of Lovers, Ring Around the Moon, Waltz of the Toreadors, The Lark*
Camus, Albert	1913-1960	*The Plague* (novel), *The Rebel* (essay), *Caligula* (play)

PAINTING

Fouquet, Jean	c.1415-c.1480	Gothic paintings and manuscript illustrations
"Maître de Moulins"	c.1480-c.1520	Franco-Flemish tradition: *Virgin and Child with Donors, St. Mary Magdalen with Donor*
Clouet, François	c.1516-c.1572	*Diane de Poitiers in Her Bath, Elizabeth of Austria*
Tour, Georges de la	1593-1652	Dramatic lighting effects and serene realism: *St. Sebastian Mourned by Women*
Poussin, Nicolas	1594-1665	Intellectual, classical works: *Shepherds in Arcadia, Funeral of Phocion*
Lorrain, Claude	1600-1682	Landscapes and mythological episodes: *Flight into Egypt, Embarkation of the Queen of Sheba*
Watteau, Antoine	1684-1721	Dreamlike, lyrical paintings: *Embarkation for Cythera, Gilles, Mezzetin*
Boucher, François	1703-1770	Decorative works for châteaux, designs for Gobelin and Beauvais tapestries, paintings of n des
Fragonard, Jean-Honoré	1732-1806	Gay, frivolous and voluptuous works: *The Love Letter, Bathers*
David, Jacques-Louis	1748-1825	Classicism: *Coronation of Napoleon, Death of Marat, Mme. Récamier, Oath of Horatii*
Ingres, Jean-Auguste-Dominique	1780-1867	Classicism: *Mme. Rivière, Odalisque*
Corot, Camille	1796-1875	Pre-impressionism: *The Port of La Rochelle, Recollection of Mortefontaine*
Delacroix, Eugène	1798-1863	Romanticism: *Massacre at Scio, Liberty Leading the People*
Daumier, Honoré	1808-1879	Satirical lithographs and oils: *Don Quixote and Sancho Panza, Third-Class Carriage*
Courbet, Gustave	1819-1877	Scenes from everyday life: *Funeral at Ornans, The Stone Breakers*
Pissarro, Camille	1830-1903	Impressionism: *The Road from Versailles to Louveciennes, The Hermitage at Pontoise*
Manet, Edouard	1832-1883	Realism and impressionism: *Déjeuner sur l'Herbe, Olympia*
Degas, Edgar	1834-1917	Impressionism: *Prima Ballerina, Carriage at the Races*
Cézanne, Paul	1839-1906	Postimpressionism: *The Card Players, La Montagne Sainte-Victoire au Grand Pin*
Monet, Claude	1840-1926	Impressionism: *Rouen Cathedral, The Seine*
Renoir, Pierre Auguste	1841-1919	Impressionism: *Le Moulin de la Galette, Mme. Charpentier and Her Children*
Rousseau, Henri	1844-1910	Primitivism; exotic jungle scenes like *The Dream, The Waterfall*
Gauguin, Paul	1848-1903	Symbolism: *The Spirit Watches, Tahitian Women with Mangoes*
Seurat, Georges	1859-1891	Postimpressionism: *Sunday Afternoon on the Island of La Grande Jatte*
Toulouse-Lautrec, Henri de	1864-1901	Poster art and illustrations, paintings of circus scenes and music halls
Matisse, Henri	1869-1954	Fauvism: *The Blue Window, Harmony in Red;* decoration of chapel at Vence
Rouault, Georges	1871-1958	Expressionism: paintings of Christ and somber clowns depicting human suffering
Dufy, Raoul	1877-1953	Light, gay horse racing and boating scenes; impressions of London and the Riviera
Derain, André	1880-1954	Fauvism, cubism and other styles; *London Bridge, Window on the Park*
Léger, Fernand	1881-1955	*Style mécanique: The City, Three Women*
Braque, Georges	1882-1963	Cubism: *Still Life with Playing Cards, Man with Guitar*
Utrillo, Maurice	1883-1955	Street scenes of Paris and environs
Duchamp, Marcel	1887-	Futurism, cubism and dadaism; *Nude Descending a Staircase*
Dubuffet, Jean	1901-	*Art brut* (raw art), stark paintings representing "a disorder of images"
Bazaine, Jean	1904-	Abstractionism: *The Flame and the Diver*
Manessier, Alfred	1911-	Abstractionism: *Crown of Thorns*, tapestry and stained glass designs

SCULPTURE

Rodin, Auguste	1840-1917	*The Thinker, The Kiss, Adam and Eve, The Burghers of Calais*
Maillol, Aristide	1861-1944	Neoclassicism: simple, massive figures of women
Arp, Jean	1887-	Bas-reliefs and sculptures with unusual tactile-visual appeal
Lipchitz, Jacques	1891-	*Man with Guitar, Mother and Child*

171

Credits

The sources for the illustrations in this book are shown below. Credits for pictures from left to right are separated by commas, top to bottom by dashes.

Cover—N. R. Farbman
8, 9—Gordon Parks
12—Chart by Bill Dove
14, 15—Gordon Tenney, Lucien Hervé
16—John Phillips
17—Loomis Dean
18, 19—A. L. Goldman from Rapho-Guillumette, C. A. Peterson from Rapho-Guillumette
20, 21—Dmitri Kessel
22, 23—N. R. Farbman
24—Loomis Dean
25—L. Sciarli from Rapho-Guillumette, United Artists
26—Alfred Eisenstaedt
27, 28—Loomis Dean
37—Gjon Mili
38, 39—Dmitri Kessel
40, 41—Loomis Dean
42, 43—Howard Sochurek, Loomis Dean
44, 45—Interpress
51—Diagram by Bill Dove
54, 55—Philip Letellier-Dalmas-Pix, *Paris-Match* from Pictorial Parade, Inc.
56, 57—Hubert Le Campion
58—Wide World Photos
59—N. R. Farbman
60—Dmitri Kessel
64—Map by Joe Kaufman
69—John Phillips
70, 71—Loomis Dean except top left Dmitri Kessel
72—Andreas Feininger—Walter Sanders
73—John Zimmerman
74—Mark Shaw

75—Ralph Crane
76, 77—Marc Riboud from Magnum, Phillipe R. Doumic from Shostal, Jerry Cooke for TIME
78, 79—Yan from Rapho-Guillumette
80—Gjon Mili
87—Edouard Boubat for *Réalités*
88—Thomas D. McAvoy
89—Joe Barnell from Shostal
90, 91—Jerry Cooke for TIME, Joe Barnell from Shostal—Gjon Mili, Walter Sanders
92, 93—William Vandivert, Thomas D. McAvoy
94, 95—Eliot Elisofon
96—Pierre Boulat
97—John Phillips
98, 99—Edouard Boubat for *Réalités*
102—Map by Joe Kaufman
106, 107—Dominique Berretty, Robert Cohen from AGIP,© Philippe Halsman
108, 109—Robert Doisneau from Rapho-Guillumette, French Film Office
110—Edouard Boubat for *Réalités*, Loomis Dean
111—Thomas D. McAvoy
112—John Phillips
119—Edouard Boubat for *Réalités*
120—Intercontinentale
121—Fonssagrives from Photo Researchers, Inc.
122, 123—Alfred Eisenstaedt
124—Courtesy The Art Institute of Chicago, Helen Birch Bartlett Memorial Collection

131—(c) Philippe Halsman
132—Brown Brothers—Courtesy John Rewald, N.Y.
133—Courtesy Courtauld Institute of Art, London—Courtesy The Cleveland Museum of Art, bequest of Leonard C. Hanna Jr.
134—Gjon Mili
135—Marie Hansen—Gjon Mili
136—Dmitri Kessel
137—Gjon Mili
138—Helene Jeanbrau
139—Robert Doisneau from Rapho-Guillumette—Gordon Parks
140—Pierre Boulat, Mark Shaw
141—Pierre Boulat—Paul Schutzer
142, 143—Eliot Elisofon, Photo *Réalités*, Jim Demetropoulos
144, 145—Scoop
150—Jean-Jacques Languepin, *Paris-Match*
151—Jo Berger
152—Evelyn Hofer
153—Yan from Rapho-Guillumette—L. Prat from Rapho-Guillumette
154—Jacques Cousteau
155—Jerry Cooke for SPORTS ILLUSTRATED
156, 157—Maurice Jarnoux for *Paris-Match*, Robert Doisneau from Rapho-Guillumette
158, 159—Mark Kauffman for SPORTS ILLUSTRATED
160—Frank J. Scherschel
165—Dalmas-Pix
166, 167—Pierre Belzeaux from Rapho-Guillumette

ACKNOWLEDGMENTS

The following scholars were of great assistance to the editors of this book: Donald M. Frame and Otis E. Fellows, each Professor of French, Columbia University, and Edward Tannenbaum, Associate Professor of History, New York University, who acted as consultants on the entire Brogan text; and Paul Beik, Professor of History, Swarthmore College, who read and commented in detail on Chapter 2.

Index

** This symbol in front of a page number indicates
a photograph or painting of the subject mentioned.*

xxxx

Production staff for Time Incorporated

John L. Hallenbeck (Vice President and Director of Production)

Robert E. Foy, Caroline Ferri and Robert E. Fraser

FRANCE
Relief Map

Canals
Rivers
△ Mountain Peaks

Cities, Towns and Villages

   1,000,000 and over
◉   500,000 to 1,000,000
⊙   50,000 to 500,000
○   50,000 and below

0 10 20 30 40 50 60 70 80 90 100 110 Miles
0 20 40 60 80 100 120 140 160 180 Kilometers

DC29 .B73   c.1
Brogan, D. W., Denis   100105 000
France, by D. W. Brogan and th

3 9810 00011726 5
GOSHEN COLLEGE-GOOD LIBRARY

COPYRIGHT BY
RAND McNALLY & COMPANY
MADE IN U.S.A.